T0169101

ATTACK THE DAY

KIRBY SMART AND GEORGIA'S RETURN TO GLORY

ATTACK THE DAY

KIRBY SMART AND GEORGIA'S RETURN TO GLORY

* * *

Seth Emerson

TRIUMPH
BOOKS

Copyright © 2020, 2021 by Seth Emerson

No part of this publication may be reproduced, stored in a retrieval system, or transmitted in any form by any means, electronic, mechanical, photocopying, or otherwise, without the prior written permission of the publisher, Triumph Books LLC, 814 North Franklin Street, Chicago, Illinois 60610.

Library of Congress has catalogued the previous edition as follows:

Names: Emerson, Seth (Sportswriter), author.
Title: Attack the day : Kirby Smart and Georgia's return to glory / Seth Emerson.
Description: Chicago, Illinois : Triumph Books, 2020. | Summary: "This book is about the Georgia Bulldogs football program" —Provided by publisher.
Identifiers: LCCN 2020018419 (print) | LCCN 2020018420 (ebook) | ISBN 9781629377230 (hardback) | ISBN 9781629375120 (ebook)
Subjects: LCSH: University of Georgia—Football. | Georgia Bulldogs (Football team) | Smart, Kirby.
Classification: LCC GV958.G44 E64 2020 (print) | LCC GV958.G44 (ebook) |
    DDC 796.332/630975818—dc23
LC record available at https://lccn.loc.gov/2020018419
LC ebook record available at https://lccn.loc.gov/2020018420

This book is available in quantity at special discounts for your group or organization. For further information, contact:
    Triumph Books LLC
    814 North Franklin Street
    Chicago, Illinois 60610
    (312) 337-0747
    www.triumphbooks.com

Printed in U.S.A.
ISBN: 978-1-62937-931-9
Design by Nord Compo
Photos courtesy of AP Images unless otherwise indicated

For Kerstin, Alex, Amelia, and Archie

Contents

Foreword

T HE KID IN FRONT OF ME WAS THIS LITTLE GUY WHO started talking to me out of the blue while we were waiting in line. This was a football camp at the University of Georgia, and they had grouped high school prospects alphabetically as we got ready to run the 40-yard dash. So I just thought this little guy was friendly, and he was, but he also had an ulterior motive, as I found out right before it was his turn to run. "Hey, big boy," the kid said. "Put your foot down right here for me, would ya?"

I did. And he used my foot as his starting block for the 40. That was my first encounter with Kirby Smart. You could see it even then: he was a competitive guy with talent and a mind at work. He was probably already plenty fast, but why not use all the tools available to you? And apparently my foot was one of them.

We would be teammates (and often classmates) for four years at Georgia on different sides of the ball. There isn't a lot of direct interaction between an offensive tackle and a safety. But even from the trenches, you couldn't help but notice and appreciate his awareness. Kirby was hyper-aware. By this I don't mean simply understanding his assignment or even everyone else's assignment. There are plenty of guys who are smart enough to know that. What I mean is he had an ability to be detail-oriented on a specific play while also understanding and seeing how it fit in the bigger picture of the game. It's the difference between knowing what to do and why you're doing it. It felt like he was always able to do that, and I think it was a big part of how he became an All-SEC defender. That and the fact that he was pretty darn good.

After our senior season, we went our separate ways. I went into the NFL, and Kirby went into coaching. A decade after we graduated, we reconnected. I was a TV game analyst for college football, and Kirby was the defensive coordinator at Alabama. Most coaches don't allow this, but when I was covering Alabama, Kirby would let me sit in on his meeting with his linebackers the Friday night before a game. I remember sitting there and being completely floored. What I saw and heard in that meeting—the amount of verbiage, checks, and adjustments—showed the system was next level in complexity. But complexity can be a disadvantage. It doesn't matter what a coach knows. What matters is what the *players* know. A slow player and a confused player look the same on film. What was remarkable was Kirby's mastery of the system and his ability to communicate it in a way where his guys could execute. I'd been around a bunch of coaches as a player and as a commentator. He stood out.

Fast forward a few years. The talk was swirling that Georgia might make a head coaching change. Mark Richt had built the program into a destination job again. That wasn't always the case. I know because I was there when it wasn't; so was Kirby. Coach Richt put Georgia back where it belonged as a national title contender. The job was going to warrant interest across the coaching landscape, and despite the fact that he had never been a head coach before, Kirby had to be considered the top target because of his background and pedigree. Besides, if you were going to be an assistant coach somewhere, Alabama was a great training ground.

The start was not a smooth one. My TV crew covered the games. So I saw firsthand when Georgia lost at home to Georgia Tech and Vanderbilt and nearly lost to Nicholls State, an FCS team. Not only did I call those games on television, but I met with Kirby in the days before. Despite the difficulties of that season—and there were more than a few—you never got a sense that it was too much, that he was sitting in a chair that he didn't belong in. It didn't seem like overconfidence either. It was more like a certainty that he knew where the program could go and how we wanted to get it there.

It was more than a cultural overhaul involving how the team practiced and changes to the offseason program. The way he was recruiting created a mass infusion of talent. That alone garners a heightened level of competition. Games are played on Saturday. They are won and lost Monday through Friday. If you can create that atmosphere where the toughest team you play most weeks is the one you face at Wednesday practice, then you have a chance at excellence.

And now look at this Georgia program. They're always on the launchpad. They're poised for a championship every year, and that's exactly where you want your program to be. That makes this a special story. Kirby's a Georgia guy. He grew up in Georgia, played at Georgia, and got his first head coaching job—maybe his only head coaching job—at Georgia. He just needs one thing to make it perfect.

—Matt Stinchcomb *was a first-team All-American offensive lineman at Georgia in 1997 and 1998. He is currently a college football analyst for ESPNU and SEC Network.*

Prologue

T HIS WAS WHERE KIRBY SMART'S ABILITY TO SURVIVE without sleep came in handy. This was the day his new job was really beginning, the first time his entire staff would be in the room together, and all their eyes would be on him as he laid out his plan and issued directives.

And he was exhausted. Or should have been.

Smart had flown in after midnight from nearly across the country, where he had for the final time coached Alabama's defense while winning another national championship. Now he turned his full attention to his next job, head coach at Georgia, and was calling everyone to the conference room in the center of the complex of staff offices.

The mood was loose, the way it usually is the first time a staff is together. Everyone spent a few minutes figuring out where everyone sat. A couple holdovers from the previous staff were unsure whether they should sit in their usual seats. The former Alabama coaches were used to sitting in certain places at a table. And the rest just looked around, waiting to take the empty seats.

Smart then came in. It had been 37 days since he had officially been given his dream job. It seemed both so long and so short a time ago. Since that day he had celebrated his 40th birthday, won a playoff semifinal, won a national title, watched Georgia win its final game without him as its coach, spoke to endless amounts of well-wishers, and put together the staff that now sat before him, awaiting his orders.

The first thing he did was outline his expectations for everyone as position coaches. There were nine of them, and almost all of them were veterans of the business who knew the basics. They already had spoken with Smart during the interview process, but it was important to Smart that he reiterate the objectives in front of the group: recruit, develop your players on and off the field, and recruit some more. Then Smart turned the meeting over to the Georgia athletic department's academic support staff, so it could explain how their side of things worked, how they worked with the players, and what the academic schedules would look like for the players. Then Smart went over each assistant coach's recruiting areas. This was something each coach probably already knew individually, but now each coach's area of responsibility was set forth for the whole group. Finally, Smart went over the schedule for the upcoming weekend. This was a Tuesday. Recruits would be coming that weekend—and the next few weekends after that. Plans had to be made. Georgia had a lot of catching up to do. The meeting then broke up. It lasted about an hour. Speaking to his entire staff for the first time, Smart did not make any momentous big-picture statements. "All business," said Shane Beamer, one of those new assistants. "Let's go."

Smart was in many ways a man caught in the middle. A decision had been made by people who ran the University of Georgia to fire his predecessor, a coach beloved by players and many in the fanbase. Mark Richt had guided the program for 15 years, lifting it to a new level in the process. But that level hadn't included a national championship, and as the fanbase watched its peers—Alabama, Auburn, LSU, Florida—win it all, they grew frustrated and felt its program was stagnant and had the wrong culture. So they had turned to the man with a compelling combination of ties: the defensive coordinator who had helped build Alabama into a powerhouse, who also happened to be a former Georgia player.

Now the hopes of a long-suffering, passionate fanbase fell upon a 40 year old who had never been a head coach before. Everywhere he went now, he was approached by fans who extended their hands and wished him luck, pleading with him to reach the promised land. You could question the expectations of the Georgia fans, but you could never question their love for their team. And there were a lot of these people. And all these people's hopes were now pinned on a head coach who was one of their own. And one of their own in more ways than just owning a diploma.

The university and alumni of Georgia are not solely geared around football. It is the endeavor that produces the most interest and unites as a guiding light, for better or worse. But the school has always been careful not to be only about football. For years it had scoffed and looked down at other schools that seemed to prioritize football over everything else, spending millions and millions while shirking academics and the welfare of others. Georgia was different. Georgia was better. It strived to be great in all areas. It could win in football while maintaining the north star of ethics and academics.

But those high ideals had been tough to maintain. The competitive gene kept kicking in as Georgia people saw their team run off the field by other programs, like Alabama, which kept winning titles while they did not. So Georgia people made their move, bringing home one of their own who had seen how it was done at one of those "other" schools. Will Leitch, an Athens resident and accomplished sportswriter, wrote the week of the coaching change in 2015 that "Georgia was now like everyone else." And that was okay as far as many in this fanbase felt. It was time to roll.

Lisa Wood was one of those fans. And two years later, after two seasons that would shape the program, Wood shared a moment that said everything about Kirby Smart.

Wood is what around the school is called a Double Dawg because she got both her bachelor's and law degree from the University of Georgia. The first woman to ever serve as chief judge for the

Southern District of Georgia, she became a federal judge appointed by president George W. Bush in 2007. She was also asked to serve on Georgia's ceremonial athletic board, which is how she found herself in the early morning hours of January 9, 2018, at the Hilton Downtown Hotel in Atlanta after Georgia had just lost to Alabama.

Wood and her husband had ridden the bus back from Mercedes-Benz Stadium with the athletic department. Other buses ahead of them were taking Georgia players and coaches to the same hotel. The mood was quiet. Georgia had fallen to dreaded Alabama in the most painful way imaginable. No one could process it yet. Everyone filed off the bus and into the hotel, said their quiet good-byes, and headed for the elevator.

Wood and her husband headed for a back area just behind the lobby, where there were two elevators. They pushed the up button but had to wait. They kept waiting. It was taking forever because players and coaches were being taken up to their rooms separately and privately so they didn't have to interact with anybody and could get to their rooms quickly. Finally, after about 10 minutes the elevator opened. They saw three people inside: two people with blazers adorned with official College Football Playoff logos—and Smart. There was an awkward pause, as nobody moved. The elevator hadn't been supposed to open. Wood's husband, who wasn't a big sports fan, didn't recognize the man a few feet in front of them. So he broke the silence: "Hey guys! Mind if we get on?"

Still not having moved, the two playoff officials just looked at Smart, who had been alone in his thoughts. He briefly snapped back to the present and nodded. "Oh, oh sure," Smart said.

Wood and her husband got on. It was dead silent as the elevator ascended floor after floor. It wasn't that long, but to Wood, it seemed like forever, so she had enough time to think of something she wanted to say. She and her husband were decked in Georgia-themed logos. Clearly, Smart knew they were fans. Wood's thoughts raced, wondering what she could say—or if she should say anything at all. She finally decided that she didn't want the last thing Smart experienced that night to be thinking that two Georgia fans were disgusted and didn't want to talk to him. Nothing could be further from the truth. The elevator came to Wood's floor first. As she and her husband got off, she turned back to the coach. "We're just getting started," she said.

She expected him to politely nod and say good night. Instead, Smart looked at her. And then he stepped toward her and off the elevator and kept looking at her as he spoke: "You've got that right!"

1

The Formative Years
of Kirby Smart

T HE FRESHMAN SAFETY SAT AT HIS LOCKER, LOOKED around at his new teammates, and had a feeling of dread. "I will never play here," Kirby Smart said to himself.

Georgia football in the mid-1990s was a largely forgettable era, a time when the program fell off the national map. Herschel Walker had left more than a decade before. Vince Dooley had stepped down in 1989, moving to the athletic director's office and handing off to Ray Goff, a popular former Georgia player who would not prove to be a great head coach. A year after Goff took over, Steve Spurrier returned to Florida and made it into the SEC's power. Tennessee under Phillip Fulmer and Peyton Manning also spiked that decade. Alabama won a national title. Georgia, meanwhile, was just kind of there. It won just five games in 1993, six games apiece the next two years, and only five games again in 1996.

This was the era, in which Smart arrived in Athens. People thought the small kid (5'10", 180 pounds) was one of the new kickers. One of the veteran safeties, Will Muschamp, practically towered over him. As Smart gazed around the locker room, all he could think about was how overwhelmed he felt. In this same locker room, Smart would one day not shrink in a locker but stand and have everyone look at him as Georgia's head coach. The formative journey to that point had already begun.

He was born in Alabama, of all places. His father, Sonny Smart, was a high school coach in Montgomery, and his mother was an English teacher. The middle of three children, Kirby was named after his great-grandfather, his mother's grandfather, who lied about his age in order to fight in World War I.

The Smart family moved across the Georgia border to Bainbridge in 1982, when Sonny got the job at the high school as the defensive coordinator. That same year Walker won the Heisman Trophy, and young Kirby Smart was smitten by the Bulldogs, running around the neighborhood in Georgia shirts and knee-high socks. Sonny would become Bainbridge High School's head coach in 1988, the beginning of a run that would include more than 100 coaching victories. His sideline manner was fairly stoic, but when needed to, he would get in a player's face. Then he would come back and pat them on the back. "The kids played for him. They loved him and would do anything in the world for him," said Goff, who would recruit south Georgia and took in more than a few games coached by Sonny Smart.

There were also the teams coached by George Bobo, who had a son, Mike, the same age as Kirby. The fathers formed a friendship across the sidelines in south Georgia, and when George Bobo semi-retired, he joined Sonny Smart's staff to help out every now and then. Their sons also became fast friends, and all they ever wanted to be was high school coaches just like their daddies.

But Kirby wasn't all about football. After all, he was the son of an English teacher, who preached academics to all three kids. The family also endured near-tragedy: Karl, the oldest child, battled lymphoma for several years, and the required treatment was hours up the road in Atlanta. The feeling of not knowing how things would turn out, the nights staying in a Ronald McDonald house next to the hospital while Karl got treatment, the entire experience would be deeply important to the family. Karl, though, got through it. His mother later wrote a long letter of thanks to the people who ran Camp Sunshine, the summer camp Karl and Kirby both attended. As a grown-up, Kirby would later read his mother's entire letter to his Georgia football team.

At Bainbridge High School, Kirby was the class president, salutatorian (just short of valedictorian), and math league MVP. He took

AP classes. An enterprising reporter for the *The Red&Black*, the Georgia student newspaper, later tracked down the class of '94 year-book, in which Kirby listed his plans upon graduation: attend UGA for football, major in business, and find a wonderful wife. His two likes were sports and winning.

For a time, it appeared Kirby may go the small-college route. Valdosta State, a tiny Division II school in south Georgia, was the first to offer him a scholarship. One of its assistant coaches, Mike Leach, later said that they thought they had a good chance to get him until bigger schools came calling like Georgia Southern, Furman, and Duke. Finally, the big school came through: Georgia, where Goff had known Sonny Smart for years, had been monitoring Kirby for awhile, especially because of his father, but had not offered a scholarship. "You knew he was a good player because he was very smart, he had good foot speed, and he knew where to be and he knew what to do," Goff said two decades later. "Based on those things, we signed him. We thought he could be a really good player. And he was!"

But Kirby had his own doubts. And when Kirby first took the field that preseason, he looked out of place. It was obvious he wasn't ready to play in the SEC yet. "I missed about 100 tackles in the scrimmage as a freshman," he said. "So I redshirted and I'm glad I did because it took me five years to graduate anyway. But I needed that extra time."

Smart was in the same class as Hines Ward, who became his good friend. It was a 26-member class, which included the usual amount of busts and what-might-have-beens. (Running back George Lombard passed on Georgia football for Major League Baseball and went on to be the first-base coach for the Los Angeles Dodgers.) When the class arrived, the ranks of veterans ahead of them included not only Muschamp, the future Florida and South Carolina head coach, but also quarterback Eric Zeier, tailback Robert Edwards, and others who went on to future success. Zeier once hazed Smart and Ward by hitting golf balls in a cement parking lot and making the two chase after them. Smart remembered thinking, *Well, if this is as bad as it gets, I'm going to be okay.*

Other veterans also took Smart under their wing. Ronald Bailey was a mentor to Smart, as well as Bailey's own younger brother, Champ. Eventually, Smart settled down on the field, and his skills starting to catch up with his knowledge of the game. "You could tell when he was a freshman that he understood the game," Goff said. "He knew what was going on, he knew what he was supposed to do, and he was able to do it."

Goff was fired after the 1995 season, Smart's first year playing, and replaced by Marshall head coach Jim Donnan, who boosted the program to a higher level, though not championship level. Smart blossomed over his final three years at Georgia, notching 13 interceptions—including two of Manning in the same game—and named first-team All-SEC in 1998. (Smart later played down that honor, saying the writers just voted for the stats, and that Smart had merely notched a lot of interceptions. And it's true that Smart wasn't the surest of tacklers at times, as some fans would later note. But he always seemed to have a great idea of where the ball was going.)

Off the field, the son of the English teacher also made an impression, though in a different academic direction. He majored in finance, graduating from the school's prestigious Terry College of Business. He also pledged Sigma Alpha Epsilon (SAE), where Smart began forming contacts he would tap into two decades later when fund-raising for facilities for his Georgia football program.

There was also the leadership part, which came easily for Smart. He was not only reared by a high school coach, but also gifted with a magnetic personality. If you watch the broadcast of Georgia's visit to then-unbeaten LSU in 1998, you can see Georgia quarterback Quincy Carter getting a pregame hand slap from a smiling Kirby Smart. This was before a game in which Carter led Georgia to victory on the offensive side, and the pivotal defensive play—knocking down a pass that would have set up LSU near Georgia's goal-line—was made by the future Georgia coach.

That play indirectly led to a set of coaching dominoes. LSU fell quickly after that loss and fired Gerry DiNardo the next year and replaced him with the head coach at Michigan State. So in that way Smart ended up causing the arrival to the SEC of his future mentor: Nick Saban.

It would still be a few years before Smart would begin his tutelage under Saban. First came a few more stops and another coach whose impact on Smart was also formative. Named head coach at the age of 26 at Valdosta State, the school where he had been the star quarterback just a few years before, Chris Hatcher was a wunderkind. Part of the reason Hatcher got the job was his contacts—his father being a high school head coach—and that led to friends at the higher levels of football. Hatcher quickly hired a defensive coordinator, Muschamp, who suggested bringing in his former teammate, Smart, who had spent his first year after graduation back at Georgia as an administrative assistant to Donnan.

Smart's interview at Valdosta State would go into disputed lore. Muschamp loves to tell the story of how Smart got in front of the staff and confidently designed a defensive play call, then stood back to let the group take it in. "Great job, Kirby, but only one problem," Muschamp responded. "You put only 10 guys on offense."

Or maybe it was 12 guys on defense. Or maybe it didn't really happen that way. In any event, Smart got the job and spent the next two years at Valdosta State, where Hatcher was in the process of building a Division II power.

Michael Doscher, who was Valdosta State's strength and conditioning coordinator back then and for the next several decades, remembered young Kirby Smart first for his humility. He had played at Georgia, been first-team All-SEC and all that, but didn't carry himself that way. Smart knew what he didn't know and wanted to learn. And he learned from Hatcher, who despite his youth knew what it took to be a head coach. "He was detailed and he was pressure-oriented," Doscher said of Hatcher. "He held his staff accountable."

Those were two attributes that would also be driven home to Smart during the Saban years. But after Valdosta State —where he was secondary coach for one season and then defensive coordinator—Smart went to Florida State to work for two years as a graduate assistant. This was one year after Mark Richt had left to become Georgia's head coach. With Richt guiding Georgia to a surprising SEC championship in 2002 and a No. 3 national ranking, Smart watched from afar as his former Georgia program rose.

Muschamp, by this time, was at LSU, having quickly risen on Saban's staff. Muschamp called Smart late in 2003 to see if he wanted to interview. Muschamp had recommended him to Saban, the hard-driving head coach who liked to surround himself with good recruiters and smart people. Smart fit the bill on both counts, Muschamp assured his boss. Saban hired Smart as his defensive backs coach, and the tutelage began—but not continuously—as it would turn out. Saban jumped to the NFL's Miami Dolphins after the season. Smart was out of a job. But then another Georgia teammate, Bobo, by then Richt's quarterbacks coach, spoke up for him. There was an opening for a running backs coach, and while Smart had never played or coached the position, everyone figured they would give it a go.

These were still the rising, great days of the Richt era. Georgia won its second—and it would turn out final—SEC championship under Richt that year. The running backs did just fine under Smart, who also spent a good part of his time traveling up to New Jersey to recruit a prospect named Knowshon Moreno. While making travel arrangements that year, Smart spent time on the phone with Mary Beth Lycett, who worked in Georgia's athletic department. Part of her job was to help with travel. Lycett had been a women's basketball player at Georgia, and the two had known each other but not well. This time they connected, began dating, and eventually married.

But the football coaching ladder was also now firmly driving Smart. He was only back in Athens that one year before Saban came calling again, asking him if he wanted to become the safeties coach with the Dolphins. Smart jumped at the chance to be at the pro level. "Georgia is my alma mater, and I can't express enough appreciation to Coach Richt, the staff, players, and the Georgia supporters for the opportunity I've had this past year," Smart said in a statement released by the school. "The position with the Dolphins came up very fast and was unexpected. However, after weighing all the factors, it's a career move that I feel I need to make."

Smart often talked about the next year in the NFL, joking about the Dolphins struggling (they went 6–10), but he also learned what it was like to be in the NFL, something he never experienced as a player. It would be over quickly. Antsy to return to the college ranks, Saban was pursued by Alabama and, after initially saying he wouldn't become its new coach, took the job. This time Saban wanted Smart to come with him. And after five stops in six years, Smart was about to settle down in—of all places—Alabama.

Joining Alabama meant something else: he would compete against Georgia, his alma mater, as well as his good friends, especially Bobo, and former boss, Richt. Georgia and Alabama may have been in separate divisions and didn't play each other every year, but they were from adjoining states, which meant recruiting a lot of the same players. That especially became the case when Smart was assigned to recruit south Georgia.

At first, Smart and his new competitors at Georgia went about everything in about as cordial a manner as they could. In fact, Bobo and Smart often arranged to carpool as they drove around the state. In retrospect it looks incredible that two rival coaches rode together as they recruited the same players, but back then it was no big deal. They drove from one school to another, often with their friend and fellow coach, Tyson Summers, and Bobo went into the high school to visit a recruit and coach while Smart waited in the car and made calls. Then Bobo came out, and Smart came in. Sometimes they weren't even recruiting the same player so it was less awkward, but often they were. Alabama and Georgia were aiming for the same caliber of recruits. "We'd go from school to school," Smart told me years later. "We never did it in Atlanta or in metro areas. We did it where we were all kind of from: up 84 across to Camilla, up to Tifton and Moultrie. We would bounce around with each other. Then at night you'd go out to dinner. You're out on the road by yourself, so it's nice to have somebody else. We always try to find out: hey, where are you stopping tonight? A lot of times when you're competing against them, you don't want to ride with them, so we would end up meeting up, whether it's in Cordele, or Tifton, somewhere off 75, eat, and share stuff."

But as the years went on, the recruiting battles became more intense. There were times that Bobo and Smart didn't speak to each other for awhile—like after Smart won the battle for highly-sought-after tailback Alvin Kamara. But after a cooling-off period, they'd be good again and then back to the recruiting battle.

Malcolm Mitchell was one such legendary battle. Mitchell was a five-star cornerback and receiver in Valdosta, Georgia, prime recruiting territory for Smart. It was basically coming down to Georgia and Alabama, and Mitchell was difficult to read. He kept things guarded and rarely did interviews. Every little thing was paramount in this recruitment. So on the first day of a legal recruiting period, Smart and a young Alabama assistant named Jeremy Pruitt concocted a way to get a leg up. "We had the grand idea we were going to sit outside his house. So when he left for school at 6:00 or 7:00, we were going to be waiting on him right then, first thing," Smart said a few years later. "Then we were going to go see him at school, then we were going to see him at practice, then we were going to see him at his house. We had this whole day planned out.

None of it seemed to matter. He still ended up going to Georgia. Coach Bobo beat us."

But the experience still taught Smart a lesson. He was still a relatively young coach and was figuring out that he didn't yet know everything. And in Mitchell, with whom Smart sat in his home, he said he never saw a kid with more respect for his mother. "I learned a valuable lesson through recruiting him. You can learn a lot about a kid's character by the way they act around their mom and the way they interact with their mom," Smart said. "He always treated her with the utmost respect. It told me a ton about the kid."

Mitchell went on to be one of the best personal stories to ever come out of the Georgia football program. After entering school with barely a sixth-grade reading level, he became such an avid reader that he joined a women's book club in Athens and wrote his own children's book. Knee injuries limited Mitchell's college and NFL career, but Smart's instincts were right when it came to his character. These were all the things that Smart was learning on his own.

The narrative is that Smart spent more than a decade at Saban's side, taking in all this knowledge from the master. And much of that is true, especially when it came to organization. (Saban had 25 more years in the business than Smart by the time they started working together.) But Saban wasn't with Smart all the time on the recruiting trail, wasn't with him in Mitchell's living room, or Kamara's high school. But obviously Smart picked up plenty from Saban, as did anybody who worked for him. He was later asked what was the biggest philosophy he picked up from Saban that he carried to this day. "The line of scrimmage wins championships," Smart answered, "and you've got to sign big football players to be successful—whether it's offensive or defensive line."

Saban also carries the reputation of being difficult to work for, but Smart managed to do it for a decade. A Georgia fan later asked how tough it was working for Saban, and Smart smiled. "Aw, that's not a tough thing. That's easy," Smart said. "It's actually great because I wouldn't be where I am today without working for Coach Saban. He is very demanding. That's great for me because I want somebody that is very demanding because I want the guy next to me putting the same sweat in the bucket that I'm putting in. So that's carried over to my staff because when you get mixed messages in there [about coaching responsibilities], you create a kind of envy in your room. [Saban] made sure there was no envy in that room. It's very straightforward about what you're supposed to do. That's the way it should be. So as far as working for Coach Saban, I think he did a great thing for my career and I learned a lot of ball from him, and there's a lot of things I've taken from him that I've learned. Now there's also things that I'm not doing that are different, but you learn that by working with somebody."

As Alabama racked up the championships and Saban cemented his position as the best coach in college football, Smart was carving his own reputation, at least in the college football industry. Smart, who Saban bumped up to defensive coordinator in 2008, quickly began popping up for head coaching jobs, first at smaller schools, then for lower-level SEC and ACC jobs, and then for higher-level jobs. Other Saban assistants came and went. Smart kept waiting before he made his next move. After the 2010 season when Georgia searched for a new defensive coordinator, the plea went out from Athens for Smart to come home. But Smart stayed in part because of Saban's persuasive powers.

By now Richt was under fire, his program having stagnated, and the risk was that Smart would be joining a sinking ship, a Georgia program whose facilities and strength and conditioning program were both lagging. Alabama, on the other hand, was a powerhouse that was still ascendant. Smart stayed put. But people in the industry kept talking about Smart. Loran Smith, the longtime Georgia historian, had conversations with contacts, including at SEC-partner television networks, who told him: "The last guys to leave the building at Alabama were Saban and Kirby."

Gary Danielson was one of those network people. The CBS color analyst gets called often by athletic directors and other people in the industry, who pick his brain on coaching candidates. Danielson had a sort of 30,000-foot view of the SEC, calling the league's best games and getting to know assistant coaches in ways that many others don't because he spent time with them before games and watched a lot of SEC practices. Danielson had watched Alabama extensively and observed Smart. "Yeah, I was pretty sure about Kirby and told a lot of people," Danielson said.

(Danielson later told people about another Alabama defensive coordinator, Pruitt, that he was also pretty sure would make a good coach. Danielson also recommended his own alma mater, Missouri, hire Gus Malzahn when he was an assistant at Auburn. That didn't materialize, at least at Missouri.)

Kevin Almond was another connection at Alabama. He was a trainer at Georgia when Goff was a player, and the two were close friends. Goff spoke a lot with Almond, who moved on to be an assistant athletic director at Alabama, and kept a special eye on the fellow Georgia graduate, Smart. "He was very optimistic for him, very high on him," Goff said. "He'd been around him for a long time and had a lot of confidence in him."

Among the other observers in Tuscaloosa was Pete Cavan, a former Alabama player under Bear Bryant whose older brother, Mike Cavan, had been a Georgia quarterback, then a college head coach, including at Valdosta State, where he recruited Hatcher.

After the 2014 season, Colorado State was among the schools that inquired about Smart, who said no thanks. The school instead hired Bobo, taking away one of Georgia's most important people. As the 2015 season began, Smart was still happy at Alabama, getting ready for another run at a national championship. It would turn out the stage had been set for this to be the year of reckoning when it came to Smart, his alma mater, and their intertwined destiny.

2

The Tumultuous 2015 Season and the End of Mark Richt

J EB BLAZEVICH LOOKED AROUND THE LOCKER ROOM. He wasn't sure what to do. His helmet sat in his locker along with his cleats and his uniform. But he didn't know whether he should put them on. The Georgia football team was supposed to hold a practice that afternoon. But Blazevich wasn't sure how they possibly could. The coaching staff was at war with itself.

The fall of 2015 was a time of countless rumors, a period of chaos that the team struggled to keep quiet. So much about the Mark Richt era had been about stability and even-keel personalities, but now in Blazevich's second year with the team, it had become the worst season—not on the field, but off it—in Georgia history. A coaching staff was torn into factions, a head coach was trying to keep the peace while his bosses were plotting his demise, and a group of players were in a daze. That included Blazevich, a sophomore tight end with a laid-back, come-what-may personality. Even he wasn't sure what to make of all of this. "We heard about a lot of stuff on the second floor," Blazevich said, alluding to where the coaches' offices were. "We'd be hearing all this drama and we were wondering: *Are we still practicing today?* How's this going to work if all this stuff is going on?"

They did practice that day and every day despite all that was going on. The coaching staff that warred in the mornings and evenings would pull it together for a few hours in the afternoon and put on a show for their players that everything was okay. But everyone knew it was not.

There were countless rumors about what was going on in real time and in the years since. The players themselves were in the dark on a lot of the rumors. The tension among the coaches was hidden during practice. Still, it was obvious something was up.

And in the end, it proved to be the end of an era, one that would usher in another one. But not before a crazy year that nobody associated with it will ever forget. "It was honestly nobody's fault," Blazevich said years later. "It was just the perfect storm for what happened. I obviously love Coach Richt and went to the University of Georgia because of him. In hindsight he would have had a lot more control over the situation. It all spun out of control so fast. Nobody knew what was happening until it happened."

* * *

Jeremy Pruitt had arrived at Georgia a year earlier to a standing ovation from his new team. He was introduced in the team meeting room on the first floor of the Butts-Mehre complex, and the team stood and cheered the new defensive coordinator. Mark Richt beamed. He had hit a home run, replacing Todd Grantham (who had jumped for a bigger contract at Louisville) by stealing away the defensive coordinator from Florida State, which had just won the national championship.

Everyone was giddy. Publicly, Pruitt gave credit to Richt for luring him, citing a meeting they'd had years before, when Pruitt walked away saying that someday he wanted to work for that great man. But in reality it was two Georgia assistants, offensive coordinator Mike Bobo and offensive line coach Will Friend, who had been the key. Friend and Pruitt had been best friends as players at Alabama, and Friend and Bobo had become close friends and convinced Pruitt to take the job. A year later, when Bobo and Friend left Georgia, the problems really started.

But in the meantime, Pruitt helped transform a Georgia program that even Richt acknowledged needed change. He was coming into his 14th year and, while he had won 75 percent of his games, five SEC East titles, and two SEC championships, he had not guided Georgia to the promised land: the national championship game. Meanwhile, Georgia fans—including influential boosters and power brokers within the administration—had watched as Alabama, under the more hard-nosed and disciplined Nick Saban, had become college football's dominant program.

So when Pruitt came to Georgia, hope came with him. He was another Saban protégé, serving as the secondary coach from 2010 to 2012 before going to Florida State for just one season. Pruitt had also worked in Tuscaloosa in one of those quality control positions, helping defensive coordinator Kirby Smart. The faction of Georgia people who clamored for Smart to return home—either as defensive coordinator or something greater—saw in Pruitt perhaps the next best thing. And very quickly it became obvious that Pruitt would try to instill that Alabama culture. It also became clear he didn't care who he ticked off along the way.

One story stuck out to Davin Bellamy above all. Bellamy was a redshirt freshman in 2014, but by the time his career was over, he would play for three different defensive coordinators. When Pruitt arrived, Bellamy saw someone who wanted to shake up the status quo. One of those places was the training room, where injured players went to rehab. It was August preseason camp of Pruitt's first year, and by about Day 13, the list of players in the training room, who would be limited that day in practice, had gotten extensive. As Bellamy put it later: "Guys were tapping out."

Pruitt was displeased. "This is why Georgia is soft now," Pruitt said, according to Bellamy. "All y'all are in the training room with bumps and bruises. This is why Georgia looks soft in the SEC."

Pruitt also did the same thing in the weight room, scoffing at players going from one set to the water fountain, one set to the water fountain, and so on. "This isn't the damn YMCA," Pruitt scolded them, according to Bellamy.

Bellamy loved it. He was a kid from the Atlanta suburbs who arrived with both a smile on his face and a chip on his shoulder, feeling he had been overlooked compared to the other recruits in the talent-rich Atlanta area. Bellamy came to Georgia because he loved the school and loved Richt and everything the coaching staff was about, but Bellamy also began to think that maybe some things needed to change.

Things did begin to change with a push from Pruitt. One rule was no water break during warm-ups. It may sound bad in this day and age of mandated water breaks, but the thinking was you only drink when you're thirsty, and you shouldn't be thirsty during mere warm-ups. Bellamy called it "training your mind."

There were other changes, such as an influx in staff. For years Georgia's administration had resisted the idea of hiring more staff than it deemed necessary, and Richt had declined to push them on it. But after Pruitt's arrival, things changed for whatever reason. Practices also became more energetic and intense, as those of us in the media could tell even during our limited viewing time.

All these changes came about not just because Pruitt pushed, but because Bobo and Friend were there and open to Pruitt's suggestions. They had more longevity and personal credibility to lobby Richt. And behind an improved defense and a record-setting offense, Georgia went 10–3, capping things off with a bowl win, in which it embarrassed Louisville and its defensive coordinator, Grantham.

But when the calendar turned to 2015, two key assistants were gone: Bobo to Colorado State as the head coach and Friend joining him as offensive coordinator. There was a voice vacuum on the coaching staff, and it would be filled by Pruitt to a large extent. There would also be a new offensive coordinator and a new strength coach and conditioning coordinator. It would all add up to disaster.

Blazevich could tell right away something was amiss. It was only the offseason, but this was a bad sign. Joe Tereshinski, a staple of the program for decades and the strength and conditioning coordinator from 2011 to 2014, had been replaced in the latter role. Mark Hocke, who had been at Alabama as an assistant strength and conditioning coordinator, was now in charge at Georgia. The strength and conditioning coordinator is one of the most important jobs in a college football program because the regular coaching staff is limited by NCAA rules in how much it can coach the players during the offseason. The strength staff, however, can interact with them liberally from January until spring practice. Once the previous season ends, the strength and conditioning program will set the tone.

Renowned as perhaps the best at his job in the country and the secret to Nick Saban's success, Hocke had served at Alabama under Scott Cochran. (Smart was also very tight with Cochran.) Pruitt, who had worked with Hocke, recommended him to Richt, who hired him, bringing in yet another Alabama transplant.

The new staff and program became a source of consternation for some players. Hocke knew the principles that had made Cochran and Alabama's program tick, but he had never been the one in charge. "I think he's learned from it and I hope he's changed," Blazevich said years later. "But he didn't know what he was doing. His support staff would even admit to us: 'I don't know what he's doing.' It was just bizarre. It just didn't make any sense."

They would get up early and run. In the weight room, players were ordered to hit a certain weight based on their position, which struck some players as counterproductive because even within position groups different guys have different goals.

There were so many meetings, and between that and the morning running sessions and weightlifting sessions, players were having trouble sleeping. Blazevich said players wondered why some of the meetings were even necessary. (Some were athletic department-type meetings, discussing how to build character and how to dress outside of sports, etc. But the football players were annoyed that some were coinciding with their schedule, overloading things.) "He just ran us into the ground. Not in a productive way," Blazevich said. "By the time we got to fall camp, we were burned out. We were sick of football."

So the year was off to a bad start before spring practice even began. That's when another problem became apparent.

* * *

Brian Schottenheimer, like Jeremy Pruitt a year before him, had been considered a coup for Georgia. After all, the school hired away the offensive coordinator of the St. Louis Rams. A few people looked at the offensive stats for Schottenheimer's teams, noticed they tended to be lower ranked compared to other NFL teams, and wondered if that was a concern. But Richt pointed out that there were only 32 play-calling jobs in the NFL, and if Schottenheimer wasn't good at his job, why did he keep getting those jobs? Yes, he was a nice guy with a famous father (Marty Schottenheimer had coached for years in the NFL without a title, sort of the Mark Richt of the NFL), but surely Brian Schottenheimer stood on his own after all these years, right?

But Schottenheimer would prove to be less like Pruitt (who kept his schemes and calls simple) and more like Todd Grantham (who had brought his NFL schemes with him). Schottenheimer came with a playbook that was just too complicated. His system was ostensibly the same type of pro-style system that Richt had always run, but that was only in name. "Schotty has an amazing playbook, but it also takes some amazing minds to make it work," Jeb Blazevich said, with a chuckle. "There were a lot of wrinkles in there but also a lot of responsibility, which is awesome, but it was just a lot to know. It was a lot to get everyone on the same page. We just didn't have the time or the energy to get out there and really fine-tune it. After practice we couldn't go out there and run another 50 plays to really get it right."

There was also the quarterback situation. Everyone expected Brice Ramsey, the strong-armed redshirt sophomore, to get the job. Richt and Mike Bobo had pinpointed him as the eventual starter when they signed him. But now Bobo, who had developed Ramsey the previous two years, was gone, and Ramsey didn't look as comfortable. As spring practice went on, Richt and Schottenheimer didn't love what they saw in Ramsey or either of the other two quarterbacks. So during the summer when Virginia quarterback Greyson Lambert decided to become a graduate transfer—meaning he was eligible right away—Richt jumped on him. Lambert would parachute in late in the summer and still win the starting job.

So to review: this Georgia team had a new strength and conditioning coordinator, a new offensive coordinator, and a new quarterback. On the one hand, it was new and exciting. On the other hand, it was false hope. Many players could tell right away. They began the year with a poor response to Mark Hocke's strength program. Then came spring practice, when Schottenheimer's playbook confused players. And as the spring went on, it also became evident that quarterback was an issue. Pruitt's defense, meanwhile, looked very good but young. Davin Bellamy remembered looking around the defense in 2015 and looking ahead to the future. The second team included himself, Lorenzo Carter, Deandre Baker, Roquan Smith, Natrez Patrick, Malkom Parrish, and others, which made for a pretty good nucleus on the second team.

The problem, everyone could tell, was the offense. Years later, Bellamy diagnosed the faults of 2015 and the successes of 2017 and beyond. "In the SEC you've got to keep it simple," Bellamy said. "And that's what Coach Smart did. In the SEC you keep it simple. Alabama keeps it simple. That's why you get the biggest linemen. You get a good running back. Teach physicality and run the ball down their throat."

The season actually started well. Georgia won its first five games. But it was a mirage. And when the schedule got tougher, the losses piled up, and the team basically imploded.

It all began against Alabama. It was the second week of October, and Alabama (4–1) came to Sanford Stadium against an unbeaten Georgia team that looked like the better team. Lambert had set an NCAA record for single-game completion percentage the second week of the season, Nick Chubb and Sony Michel led the backfield, and Pruitt's defense was flying around. Georgia was even slightly favored by the Las Vegas books. In the lead-up to the game, *USA TODAY* ran a story quoting Georgia boosters on how happy they were with Richt and the program and the perception that their way—The Georgia Way—was better for their school than the perceived Alabama way.

Nick Saban, Kirby Smart, and his players arrived in Athens on Friday as is customary. They arrived with a weather system that would bring a cold rain to the game a day later. But it was still sunny about an hour before kickoff when Alabama took the field, and Smart, wearing a white pullover jacket, looked around at the stadium, in which he had played and smiled. It was almost as if he knew something.

The game wasn't close. Alabama embarrassed Georgia 38–10. Through a combination of the score and the weather, most of the crowd was gone as the fourth quarter trudged on. The Bulldogs' season had begun its slide.

A week later Georgia took a 24–3 lead at Tennessee only to blow it and lose 38–31. Making matters even worse, Chubb tore up his knee on the first series of the game. After squeaking by Missouri at home in a 9–6 field-goal fest, Georgia had a bye week before the trip to Jacksonville against Florida, a game that would decide whether the season could be salvaged. This was the time to regroup and reassess the offense. And that's just what Richt and Schottenheimer did.

After that great start, Lambert had been uneven, and Brice Ramsey had struggled when put in as the backup. So the coaches debated whether to mix things up and put in the third-stringer, Faton Bauta, a redshirt junior who did not have a strong arm but was athletic. Loved for his spirit and work ethic, Bauta was also a favorite of his teammates.

The decision to start Bauta was ultimately Richt's to make, though there was support on the coaching staff, including from Pruitt. The surprise move was kept secret until the day before the game, when word finally began to leak out. Todd Gurley and other former Georgia players now in the NFL tweeted out their support, loving the fact that Bauta was getting his shot.

Others were more confused. "They're not really doing this, are they?" Florida athletic director Jeremy Foley said in the press box before the game to a few media members. He was smiling.

They were doing it. And fair or not, Bauta's struggles—four interceptions, one of which bounced off a receiver's hands and at least one more where a receiver ran the wrong route—became symbolic for the season. Georgia lost 27–3, and Bauta would never start again at Georgia.

Richt's fate was sealed. Georgia's administration began making its plans, especially after catching wind that a division rival was sniffing around the Georgia boy in Tuscaloosa. As for those still at Georgia, it would only get worse.

Rumors were everywhere. Players were hearing them as much as the public was.

"At the end of the year, we knew Richt was out of there. We didn't *know*, but we knew," Bellamy said. "You could have cut the tension with a knife in the Butts-Mehre...But [the coaches] did a great job of keeping the team focused."

It took great effort.

There were cliques on the coaching staff. There was Pruitt and his group: Kevin Sherrer, Tracy Rocker, Rob Sale, the people on the support staff whom Pruitt had helped bring in. Mike Ekeler, the odd man out among the defensive coaches, grew more bitter at the situation as the season went on. There were Thomas Brown and Bryan McClendon, who were Richt loyalists in the best sense, having been recruited by Richt as players. Schottenheimer, a first-year coach trying to figure out his new place, was kind of on his own. And then there was tight ends coach John Lilly just doing his best to keep his head down. He would tell his tight ends: "I'm here for you all to help us do this."

In retrospect, the departure of Bobo and Will Friend had been the undoing. Richt loyalists who were close friends with Pruitt, the two could straddle both worlds. Both had the ability to calm Pruitt down while also agreeing with him. Bobo, in particular, as a Georgia graduate who knew everyone in the building, could smooth over a lot of things. But when the pair left for Colorado State, there was no one to jump into those roles. Lilly and McClendon were also popular with everybody and low key, but they were only position coaches.

It was Pruitt who filled the power vacuum even more. That might not have been a bad thing, as he seemed to have the right ideas and the desire to put the Alabama/Saban imprint further on the program. But Pruitt had rougher edges, and without Bobo and Friend there to play good cop, the fissures started to explode. It was a weird tension that Blazevich, looking back, thinks he would recognize now but didn't in the moment. "From my point of view, that was the worst year," Blazevich said. "Just in terms of physically, mentally, and emotionally draining, that was one of the worst years period."

One possible reason for the team's collapse in October was the practice schedule. Starters were getting more tired as the season went on, according to Blazevich. The first team and third team would get six plays each in a period, and the second and fourth-string would get two plays. The offensive starters were gassed, and it led back to the problems with Hocke and the strength program. "That's really where it started to crumble was the lack of trust in him, which led to a lack of trust in the play calls, which led to this really rough tension," Blazevich said. "And there was a lot of drama with the coaches."

Even years later, the exact nature of that drama is still hard to pin down. There are stories of confrontations, but sources maintain there were no actual fistfights. After the 2015 season ended, Tracy Rocker alluded to a "mutiny" on staff. Ekeler, speaking the next year, told the *North Texas Daily*: "What it boils down to is people. You can be at the University of Georgia and be miserable if you're working with shitty people."

Many in Georgia's administration, meanwhile, had particular disdain for Pruitt, who had first aroused their ire late in the 2014 season by passive aggressively criticizing the lack of a full-length indoor facility. (Georgia, incredibly, was the only team in the SEC not to have one.) Behind the scenes—unafraid to say what was on his mind, whether it was to underlings, administration, or other athletic department staffers—Pruitt's edges were just as rough.

But somehow, as things were unraveling off the field, the team rallied on the field. Georgia went unbeaten down the stretch, needing overtime against Georgia Southern to do it, but it still did it. Richt's even-keel approach may have hurt the team's ability to win big games, but it helped keep it together even when his fate, whether he knew it or not, was fait accompli. "That was honestly the best we played because we were like: 'All right, forget all the coaching drama. Forget what people are saying. Let's just do what we do. Let's go have fun,'" Blazevich said. "'We know what's going on. Things are weird, but forget everyone else. We don't care what they say. We're here for one another.' That's when we bonded as a team, but it was out of that tension."

On a cold but sunny day at rival Georgia Tech in the last game of the season, this Georgia team won its third straight game. Georgia players celebrated by planting the Georgia flag at midfield. They felt good about what they had done. And players, at least some of them, claimed that their coach's job status should be a non-issue now. "I'm surprised people were even talking about that," senior linebacker Jordan Jenkins, the senior outside linebacker, said after the game. "This should end that."

But in fact the decision had already been made. Change was coming.

3

The Power Brokers Hire Kirby Smart

M IKE CAVAN WALKS AROUND WITH A PERPETUAL smile, often dressing down in a pullover and sweats. He doesn't carry himself like one of the most consequential people in Georgia football history. But there's a good argument that he is. "He means so much to the university," Kevin Butler, the former Georgia kicker and college football Hall of Famer, said. "He's responsible for getting Kirby to Georgia. I don't know if he gets due credit on that, but there's no one more responsible for getting Kirby than Cavan. He's been great for the university."

A former Georgia starting quarterback, Cavan had a modest playing career from 1968 to 1970 during an era where Vince Dooley's team mostly ran the ball. But Cavan led Georgia to the SEC championship as a sophomore. Then Cavan went into coaching, where he rose to the head coaching ranks also with modest success. His teams at Valdosta State (Division II), East Tennessee State (Division I-AA), and SMU went a combined 89–83–2. The SMU stint was the most notable. With the notorious program still reeling from the NCAA death penalty, Cavan trudged through in five years there, going 22–34 before being let go and seemingly disappearing from the coaching landscape.

But Cavan did not disappear. He began a second career as a mover and shaker behind the scenes. Cavan had the personality and the connections to be a power broker. But he also had the credibility thanks to one name: Herschel Walker.

Even before the age of the Internet, Walker was a mega-recruit out of Wrightsville, Georgia. Every major college wanted him, and it was no guarantee that Georgia, which was coming off a 6–5 record in 1979 and was four years removed from its most recent SEC championship, would get the homegrown star. By this time a Georgia assistant, Cavan became Walker's lead recruiter. Cavan literally moved into Walker's neighborhood and eventually helped secure the commitment of the best player in Georgia football history. "He was the most loyal and enthusiastic coach we ever had. He was always full of personality and a great recruiter —just ask Herschel," Vince Dooley said of Cavan in his book, *Dooley: My 40 Years at Georgia.*

So when Cavan left coaching and returned to Athens, he was a natural fit in Dooley's athletic department in an off-the-field role. He was hired in development, a fancy word for fund-raising. Through that job Cavan made more connections and also gained the freedom of movement within the athletic department, getting involved in decisions but not pushing his way into things. (I remember a day I was with Greg McGarity at his office on the fourth floor of the Butts-Mehre, and Cavan walked in holding a printout of a sordid story at another SEC school, saying something along the lines of: "Well, this is pretty interesting, isn't it?" It impressed upon me how Cavan literally had the walk of the halls of power in the football facility.)

Cavan, like most people, liked and supported Mark Richt for most of his tenure. But Cavan was among those who also grew weary of his falling short on the field and envious of what Nick Saban had built at Alabama. And Cavan, like most people, also was well aware that Alabama's defensive coordinator was Kirby Smart. Cavan is 27 years older than Smart, but they had plenty in common. They were both the sons of successful high school coaches, both had grown up in south Georgia, both played at Georgia, and both even coached at Valdosta State.

Cavan was also a Richt loyalist for a long time, according to one knowledgeable booster, even up to the start of the fateful 2015 season. But like many he became more exasperated as the season went on, culminating with the loss to Florida. At halftime of that game with Georgia trailing 20–0 and the Faton Bauta experiment already a failure, Cavan walked into a room with several boosters. "I can't defend this anymore," he said, according to someone in the room.

As the discontent with the Richt era built to a crescendo in 2015, Cavan became a sort of focal point for the power brokers, someone who could reliably pass on the concerns and have the right conversations. Cavan would probably downplay all that or even deny it. There's a protocol for hiring football coaches. But more than a few people around the program spoke of Cavan as the connective tissue—whether it was because of his brother Pete being in Tuscaloosa, Alabama; Cavan knowing Smart himself; or his status within Georgia's athletic department as someone with the ear of the administration as well as the most influential boosters. "Every story I know—and I know a lot of stories—Mike Cavan set it up, Mike Cavan had the relationship with Kirby," Butler said. "Certainly, when it came to the meeting with Greg [McGarity] and Kirby, that was Mike. Mike knew we needed to act, and we needed to act quickly because Kirby was, first of all, the best guy for the job hands down, and, secondly, that his clock was ticking. He was ready to be a head coach. I think everybody certainly realizes that. Mike certainly wasn't sitting there not liking Mark. He had a wonderful relationship with Mark, but times were changing. We knew it was going to change. And anytime you change, you better have a plan, and Georgia had a plan. That's what I think put everything into motion."

There had long been murmurs of discontent about how things were going under Richt. Now things were turning full steam. Influential power brokers, including Don Leebern Jr. (a powerful member of the Georgia Board of Regents), saw Florida as the breaking point. The decision was basically already made by the Georgia Southern game, which saw Georgia need overtime to win, and the ensuing celebration irked those power brokers again.

Georgia staffers sensed it when they returned to Athens. People stopped coming around. They stopped receiving encouraging texts and calls. The atmosphere was frosty. Richt also realized he was in trouble. In a valiant move to save his job, or at least to show the fanbase he was dedicated to turning things around, he went on a surprise—and public—recruiting tour. First was to Washington state, where on the day after the win over Auburn, the Twitterverse was shocked to see a photo pop up in their feed: Richt and Jacob Eason sitting at a breakfast table. Richt had flown all the way out after the game. It was seen in some quarters as a power play move by Richt against the forces against him—even the ones at his own school. Let me go, Richt was saying, and you risk losing Jacob Eason.

Publicly, Richt played that down. In his normal Sunday evening teleconference with reporters, he brushed it off, saying he wanted to focus on Georgia Southern, the next opponent.

But as Richt spoke, an intercom could be heard over him. He was still at the airport. And he was flying commercial. In hindsight, it would be yet another sign of what was to come.

There was another factor in all this. South Carolina had an opening because Steve Spurrier had suddenly retired midway through the season. And the scuttlebutt was that the Gamecocks had zeroed in on a target: Smart. The feeling among more than a few people at Georgia was *We can't let that happen*. Whether South Carolina's search prodded Georgia into making its coaching change is also something Georgia people will tread carefully on if not outright deny, but a clue was laid the following spring by Tyler Simmons, who in the fall of 2015 was a receiver in Powder Springs, Georgia. He had committed to Alabama, and his main recruiter was Smart. "By this time he knew he was going to get a head coaching job," Simmons told me the following spring. "He just didn't know where yet. He told me beforehand, 'If you commit [to Alabama], if I get a head coaching job somewhere else, I'm coming for you.'"

That's exactly what ended up happening, and Simmons ended up playing a pivotal role in one of Smart's most pivotal games. But first came the coaching change itself, which did not come without its share of drama.

*   *   *

Georgia's locker room was ebullient after beating Georgia Tech. At least the players. The coaches were trying to put on a brave face, but they knew something was coming. They couldn't help but notice who wasn't in there with them. School president Jere Morehead. Greg McGarity. They had normally been in the postgame locker room, especially after this game. McGarity had briefly shaken hands with Mark Richt as the coach came off the field, then walked the length of the track around Georgia Tech's field, and headed to his car to drive back to Athens. Morehead was nowhere to be seen either. The governor of Georgia, Nathan Deal, and a few staffers were in the locker room. They, along with the head of Children's Healthcare in Atlanta, were there to present the Governor's Trophy. But the absence of Richt's bosses was conspicuous. "I remember thinking, *This isn't good*," one person in the locker room said. "On the university's totem pole, the highest-ranking person in that locker room was Mark Richt."

But not for long. Richt fielded a call Sunday morning from McGarity, asking to meet that morning. Richt knew what that meant. If he wasn't being fired, then the meeting could have been later in the day or later in the week. When they met, McGarity gave Richt the option of how to phrase the dismissal in the press release and whether he wanted to coach in the bowl. They agreed upon his stepping down after the bowl game, very flowery language about Richt's time at Georgia, and his continuing on to run the Paul Oliver Network, which was Richt's passion project for former players.

But everyone understood the deal.

The players found out—or at least were supposed to find out—via a text message sent out to all of them later that morning. But players get a lot of text messages and often don't check them, especially on a Sunday morning. Jeb Blazevich found out about Richt's firing from a phone call from a friend. "Sorry about Coach Richt," his friend said.

"What?" Blazevich said.

"Oh, yeah, he got fired."

"Cool, cool, great," Blazevich said, in an eye-rolling fashion.

The story broke quickly after that. ESPN's Mark Schlabach, a former Georgia beat writer for *The Atlanta Journal-Constitution*, tweeted the news. Chaos broke very quickly—or at least it did online. In Athens things were pretty quiet. When I went to the Butts-Mehre facility to begin what turned out to be a very long stakeout, the only player I initially encountered was offensive tackle John Theus, who was filling up his scooter at the gas station across the street. Theus shrugged, calmly told me how they'd found out, and didn't betray much feeling either way. He was a senior on his way out anyway.

But some players did get fired up after a team meeting that night. About a dozen media members, including myself, were there to stake them out. While a few players avoided us as best they could, a few wanted to talk. Jordan Jenkins, a senior outside linebacker, was particularly animated. "It ain't right," Jenkins said, looking down and walking but speaking loudly. "Ain't no Georgia football without Coach Richt. Just the way he dealt with everybody up here. And the way it went down, just don't sit right just from what we've been hearing. We're meeting with McGarity tomorrow, but it's just messed up."

Leonard Floyd, another star outside linebacker, was also ticked. So much so that he used the occasion to declare for the NFL draft. Floyd was in a car with some teammates when, after driving by some media members, he ordered the driver to stop the car. Floyd leaned out the window and yelled to the media: "I'm gone!"

But while there was plenty of anger, deep down there was also an acknowledgment that it wasn't working anymore. "I knew it was time for a change," Davin Bellamy told me years later. "It was time for a change, time for a fresh start. We were kind of stalemated, just coming to the building, our same routine every day."

An image from that Sunday night that I'll never forget may have summed it up best. Walking alone through the atrium in the facility, wearing a black Georgia track suit, putting his finger on a scanner to get to the coaches' offices, Richt walked in. He was alone and he seemed to be at peace.

* * *

The reports about Kirby Smart emerged almost right away. Chip Towers put out a report that afternoon quoting someone as saying in effect that this was all about getting Smart. But other conflicting reports came out. Dan Mullen, then the head coach at Mississippi State, got more than a few mentions. The signs, though, pointed heavily to Smart, who was getting ready for the SEC championship that week in Atlanta. By Tuesday night Towers had heard enough to feel good about writing that Smart would be the next coach. It was quickly confirmed by others.

Gary Danielson, the CBS color analyst, also saw a change coming down the pike at Georgia. And he was among those who thought Smart and Georgia were the perfect match.

"I always thought that Georgia was...it's not that it wasn't perfect before. But I thought it had more potential. I always did," Danielson said. "That's not to say anything bad because I don't like to talk that way, but I always thought Kirby could win in the right spot. And it turned out to be the right spot."

Ray Goff, the coach who first brought Smart to Georgia more than two decades before, watched the move happen and approved. It was the right combination: someone who would bring the Nick Saban model but also knew Georgia enough to tweak it where needed. "Anytime you're around somebody as long as he was Coach Saban, there's still a lot that you want to take with you but also there's a few things that you want to instrument," Goff said, speaking a few years later. "I don't think everything he does has been done at Alabama. He's got his own set of rules that he wants to live by and go by, and I admire him for that."

When it looked like Smart could be the new head coach, the reaction among many players was immediate: *That sounds great. Keep Pruitt since he's also an Alabama guy.* "We know he's a great coach, but we like Pruitt," Bellamy said, summing up his feelings at the time. "We were a top 10 defense under Pruitt, so I don't see why we're making a change, and that's how everybody was."

The defensive players began a "Keep Pruitt" campaign. They tweeted it, and freshman safety Jonathan Abram voiced it the night of Richt's firing when he spotted media members in the parking lot, staking out the players' meeting with Richt. "If the media wants to know anything," Abram said as he walked by, "tell them to keep Pruitt."

There was no chance of that because of the Georgia administration's strained relationship with Pruitt. *Strained* was a nice way of putting it. But the players didn't know that, and while even some of Pruitt's defensive players didn't like him, the majority did. They saw themselves as "Pruitt's babies," as Bellamy put it, including those not recruited by him like Bellamy. That's another reason Smart proved to be a healing choice. He would be seen as an extension of Pruitt, softening the blow of a beloved (in some quarters) defensive coordinator not being retained.

Smart's hiring became official the Sunday morning after the SEC championship. It had been unofficial for some time. There were half-hearted attempts to make it look like it had happened between the time Alabama won the SEC championship and when the Georgia Athletic Board met the following day. But if anyone thought Smart would accept a job—and let it leak, as it had earlier in the week—without first taking a meeting with his new employer, then they were kidding themselves. And Jimmy Sexton, the agent to the college football coaching stars, including Smart, had been doing this a long time. He knew how to play the game.

When media members spotted Sexton in the hallway at the Georgia Dome, Sexton bolted. Smart also gave the media the slip out of Alabama's locker room. He went off to meet with the Georgia people, including President Morehead, and made it official over that night and the next morning, signing what needed to be signed.

Smart was introduced to the team on Monday morning. First, athletic director Greg McGarity came in and said a few words. Then Smart went to the podium. He spoke about needing to get to know each one of them and that they would hold individual meetings introducing the staff, etc. He also told the team why he would not be joining them full time until Alabama's playoff run was over. "I made this commitment to Alabama if they were going to make a championship run. If they weren't in the playoffs, it might be different. But we're in the playoffs, so I want to finish this out," Smart said, according to Jeb Blazevich.

Players understood and took well to that.

Nearly every Georgia player already knew who Smart was well before he was hired. He had recruited many of them, either intensely or at least just once. And those who hadn't been recruited by him tended to be aware that Alabama's defensive coordinator was a Georgia alum.

During the recruiting process, Smart had even made a somewhat joking comment to a few of them. When he encountered Jonathan Ledbetter, the two embraced, and then Smart's eyes lit up.

"I told you I was going to come back and coach you, didn't I?" Smart said, according to Ledbetter.

The two laughed. Ledbetter was only a freshman with three more years of eligibility and much personal adversity about to come his way. But looking back years later, he saw the moment of Smart's introduction as a clear moment in time. "I knew the whole culture was about to transform," Ledbetter said. "I knew it was going to be totally different, and it was going to be for the better. And everyone else did too."

Smart also came in with immediate credibility with players. For some, the fact he had played at Georgia helped. (But Smart didn't bring that up too much.) For some, it was that they had come to know him during recruiting. But for most, the fact he was able to flash those championship rings—and they knew he had learned under Saban—was the biggest deal. "You've gotta realize, too, man, he learned from a great on how to run a program," Bellamy said. "He was his right-hand man. I feel like with Kirby he waited for the perfect time. He earned his wings. And when it was time to drive his own ship, he drove it and he's driving it damn good."

Smart's introductory press conference was held Monday morning. He appeared nervous. Limited to twice-a-year interviews at a podium by Saban, Smart wasn't very used to public speaking, but he was able to look out at the audience and not only see Mary Beth and their three children but his parents and former Georgia teammates like Dax Langley, Travis Stroudt, and Corey Allen. "I've thought about this day all of my life," Smart told the crowd. "As the son of a high school coach and the best English teacher in the world, I've always aspired to be a head coach. Thanks, Mom, thanks, Dad, for the example you set for me and for so many others. As most of you know, I spent five of the greatest years of my life here in Athens as a student-athlete. As I look throughout this very storied program, there are several coaches that had a great impact on my life here."

Then he name-checked the coaches who preceded him: Vince Dooley (also in the audience), Goff, Jim Donnan, and Mark Richt. Then he called out his wife, Mary Beth who, as he pointed out, was also a former Georgia student-athlete. The prepared statement was relatively brief. Then Smart opened it up for questions. The audience listened while reporters asked questions. They were mostly quiet except for one spontaneous moment, which said so much.

A reporter asked Smart whether he would be hands on with the defense rather than just leaving it to his assistants. It was a rather innocuous question, but Smart took it another way.

"Oh no," he said, "I'm hands on with the whole program. I'm hands on with *everything.*"

There was a small eruption or claps and "yeahs" from the audience. The meaning was clear. A segment of the fanbase, perhaps a large part, had grown tired of Richt's CEO approach, a detachment they thought had cost them in the race to equal the detail-oriented Saban. Now they had someone more like Saban. And Smart would spend the next few months and years showing that wasn't just talk. But first he had a plane to catch.

4

Building His Program

K IRBY SMART MAY HAVE BEEN SEEN AS THE NEW STEW-
ard of the Georgia program. But if anyone was considered, at
least at the time, the actual savior of the program, it was not Smart.
It was Jacob Eason. And now Eason was a free agent.

The five-star quarterback had not officially de-committed
from Georgia. But both the head coach who had recruited him
to Georgia, Mark Richt, and his main recruiter initially to Georgia,
Mike Bobo, were elsewhere. Eason, the savior of the program, was
now clearly available, and another school—Florida—was trying
very hard.

Smart was barely on the job—and actually still had another
job—but this was a huge early test, and he was not going to shirk
from it. After Smart's hiring was announced, offensive lineman Ben
Cleveland had been the first prospect he visited that Sunday night
because Big Ben was down the road. But Smart had also made sure
to book a flight as soon as possible to go to Washington state. And
so began a frenzied first 10 days on the job, in which he flew across
the country and back, hired two of his most important coaches, got
jilted by one of his best friends, and won his first recruiting battle
after some drama on an airport tarmac.

Smart's trip to see Eason went well. The quarterback himself
wasn't actually wavering that much. He had really liked Richt and
Bobo, but he also loved the idea of playing in the SEC and had
loved Georgia's campus. He also had a loyal streak. It was his father,
Tony Eason, a former Notre Dame receiver, who needed a bit more
convincing but only for practical reasons. Smart came off great
when he met the family, but who would be his offensive coordinator? I'm working on that, Smart told the family, in so many words.

There's always a list of coaching candidates in the minds of aspiring head coaches. Smart, who had interviewed at big and small schools alike over the years, always had that list. Bobo was at the top of it at some points, especially when Smart was close to getting the Auburn job in 2012. But Bobo was now a head coach himself. And retaining Brian Schottenheimer was not an option. The search would likely go beyond his inner circle. Smart only knew he wanted someone who would run his preferred style of offense, one like Alabama and Georgia ran, and who would emphasize the run. SEC experience was preferred, if not a must.

Arkansas offensive coordinator Dan Enos was on Smart's radar screen. As a courtesy Smart called Arkansas coach Bret Bielemma, who was able to cut off the conversation very quickly. Enos had a non-compete clause in his contract, and Bielemma didn't let him go. Smart said thanks and hung up, and the self-satisfied Bielemma felt so good about being able to stave off someone trying to raid his staff that he let local media know what had happened. But there was something else Bielemma didn't know: Smart was coming for one of his other coaches, who didn't have a non-compete.

Sam Pittman was beloved by almost everyone. He was a laid-back Oklahoman, who had played small-college ball, become an offensive line coach, and become one of the best in the business at it. He had worked his way up through the ranks and coached offensive lines at 10 different stops at the FBS level. In his third year at Arkansas, he had built one of the better lines in the conference. Pittman's reputation was as a great recruiter and a good coach, a combination that made him one of the most respected in his craft in the country and very attractive to Smart, whose defenses had gone against Pittman's lines the past four seasons, including in 2012 when Pittman was at Tennessee.

Pittman also had a connection. He was close with Jim Chaney. The two had worked together at Missouri, Tennessee, and Arkansas before Chaney left to become the offensive coordinator at

Pittsburgh. The two weren't necessarily a package deal, but they loved working together. And Smart had the checkbook to lure them together to Georgia.

Pittman and Chaney spoke to Smart that week and spoke to each other. By Friday a deal was struck. It wasn't hard for Georgia to top what Pittsburgh was offering. And to get Pittman, Georgia offered him not only a raise, but also a three-year contract, unprecedented for a mere position coach at the time. Arkansas would not let Pittman go easily. His offensive linemen, who got wind of what was happening, went to his house that night. Some begged him to change his mind, and others just wanted to hear it straight from Pittman. The common theme was mutual love. There was crying. "He was upset about it," Zach Rogers, then an Arkansas offensive lineman, told me a couple years later. "He told us he was going. He felt like he needed to go. But it felt like he was sad to leave us, too. It's not like he was all 100 percent excited getting away from all of us. It was a pretty personal thing to him, too."

It sucked, as Rogers put it, but it was also "just all part of the college football business."

The Georgia plane arrived in Fayetteville and Pittsburgh on Saturday morning and flew them back to Athens. Smart was wasting no time putting them to work, especially Chaney, who had a key recruit to meet.

* * *

Jacob Eason had visited Florida earlier that week. Other schools had lit up his and his father's cell phone, but it was pretty clear that if Eason was going anywhere else, it was to Florida. Head coach Jim McElwain—another former Alabama and Nick Saban assistant—and offensive coordinator Doug Nussmeier had good reputations. Georgia, meanwhile, didn't even have an offensive coordinator.

47

Jim Chaney's hiring changed that, and within minutes of his arrival in Athens, he was put in front of Eason, who was now back in Athens for an official visit. He and his family didn't want this thing to linger very long. And now they could sit down with the man who would be his position coach and coordinator for the next three-to-four years (or so they assumed) and make a decision. By the end of the trip, the family was back on board. They still wanted him to go to Georgia.

But Florida wasn't giving up easily. Georgia's staff drove Eason to the Atlanta airport and figured they were in the clear because the following day was the start of a dark period, when coaches could no longer contact recruits. What they hadn't counted on was Nussmeier being at the airport, too. The plan was to book a flight to go with him, fly out to Washington with him, and flip him before the dead period began the next day—or at least have him postpone his decision.

But Christine Eason, the player's mother, was having none of it. They were done. It was going to be Georgia, the Gators delegation was told in so many polite words. They went back to Gainesville, Florida. After thinking it over just a little more on the flight to the West Coast, Jacob Eason called Kirby Smart on Monday evening to re-affirm his commitment and then he officially announced it the next day.

It was a critical early win for Smart. Richard LeCounte actually had been the first player to commit to Smart's program, doing so on December 14, 2015. He was a five-star recruit at the time and was a very good start, but he was also an in-state player seen as a Georgia lean anyway and someone the previous staff had recruited. LeCounte was also a junior who would not play until 2017.

Eason was the big prize. "Kirby winning that battle, that held a lot of things together," recruiting analyst Rusty Mansell said, looking back years later. "Regardless of what happened, Eason was a guy that people wanted to go play with. He was liked by a lot of these recruits. And he held on in a short time. So I think in the short term, Jacob Eason was a huge recruit for showing people that Kirby could hold things together, and he was going to be able to keep this deal together."

Mecole Hardman, Isaac Nauta, and others signed on shortly afterward. And as the team put together the 2017 recruiting class, the allure of playing with Eason could only help.

It didn't get as much notice, but the same day that Eason re-affirmed his commitment to Georgia, another high school quarter-back backed off his commitment. Bailey Hockman, whom Mark Richt and Brian Schottenheimer had talked into committing for the 2017 class a year after Eason, announced he was no longer commit-ted to Georgia. That news opened the door to another quarterback in the 2017 class, one who eventually chased Eason out of Athens. But no one could know that at the time.

Smart had all these early wins in his first week-plus on the job. But he would take a loss, too. It was well-known that he was close with Scott Cochran, Alabama's longtime strength and conditioning coordinator, who had been cited as the secret to Saban's success. He had become a cult hero to Crimson Tide fans. And when Smart was hired, there was plenty of buzz that Cochran was coming with him—buzz that Smart began to defuse at his press conference.

"I don't know if Scott Cochran is coming," Smart said in a way that indicated real lack of certainty rather than coyness.

But Smart and Georgia did make a good offer. At one point Cochran was ready to make the move. But then he met with Saban, who was armed with persuasive power—such as a better weight room at Alabama than Georgia—and the promise of a raise.

Alabama announced the news that Cochran was staying on Monday night, the same evening that Smart heard from Eason that he was coming. That set the tone for the next few years. Smart could beat out the Gators, but his old team would be tough to beat. And yet Smart, in going to Plan B for a strength and conditioning coordinator, ended up hitting a home run anyway.

Putting together his own staff was a new experience for Smart. He had sat in on interviews at Alabama, but ultimately every call belonged to Saban. Now every call belonged to Smart, who was adjusting to a new role.

A few of the hires were easier than others. Mel Tucker came with Smart from Alabama, where he had been the secondary coach the past year, and took that job at Georgia, as well as defensive coordinator. Tucker's background was mainly in the NFL, where at one point he had been the interim head coach for the Jacksonville Jaguars, but mostly he had been a defensive coordinator. Georgia's new head coach was, well, *smart* enough to know what he didn't know, and by having veterans at both coordinator spots, there would be less of a sense of learning on the job.

Glenn Schumann was another guy Smart wanted to bring with him. Although Tucker was an experienced veteran, Schumann was only 25 and had just been an analyst. But he had obvious communication skills and helped Smart behind the scenes. Schumann would become the inside linebackers coach. The other two defensive spots were filled by two Georgia holdovers: defensive line coach Tracy Rocker and outside linebackers coach Kevin Sherrer. Smart knew Sherrer from Alabama, and Rocker's reputation was already well established.

Initially, running backs coach Thomas Brown was going to be retained as well. Smart had actually coached Brown on the 2005 Georgia squad, when Smart was the running backs coach. But after a few weeks of recruiting for Smart and Georgia, things changed. Richt had become the University of Miami head coach and had kept pursuing Brown, who eventually decided to follow his former head coach. Smart wasn't pleased to lose Brown, but much like missing out on Cochran, it worked out just fine.

Dell McGee, who had been the running backs coach at Georgia Southern, was well known in the state of Georgia, having coached Carver High School in Columbus to state titles. That gave McGee a huge rolodex of recruiting contacts, and Smart couldn't resist that possibility. McGee went on to become an elite recruiter for Georgia.

James Coley had been somebody that Smart had on his radar screen for offensive coordinator. But it would have been a reach. Coley's time as the play-caller for Miami coincided with a slip in the program, culminating in the firing of head coach Al Golden during the 2015 season. Many around Miami's program didn't blame Coley, who didn't have much of an offensive line or a running game, and the defense struggled. Coley was also a well-known recruiter in the south Florida area, and Georgia needed someone with a foothold there, especially with Richt heading the Miami program.

Smart and Coley knew each other well. They had worked together at LSU in 2004 and the Miami Dolphins in 2006 both times under Saban. Although Smart had someone else to fill the offensive coordinator spot for that first Georgia staff, he filed away what he knew about Coley's time at Miami, and that would become useful down the road.

Finally, there was Shane Beamer, who, like Coley and McGee, was a coaching free agent. Beamer's father, Frank, had retired after a legendary tenure at Virginia Tech. And although Shane Beamer and Smart had never worked together, their relationship showed how small the coaching fraternity can be. They knew each other through Mike Bobo, who, like Smart, seemed to know everybody. When Beamer was a student at Virginia Tech, he had a friend who lived above him who knew Bobo, and when all three of them got into SEC coaching at the same point, they ran into each other at events. Beamer's father also had a house on Lake Oconee, Georgia, where Smart also eventually bought a house, and so the relationship took off from there. Smart, Beamer, and Bobo occasionally golfed together, and Beamer sometimes called Smart to pick his brain on football matters. When Beamer was at Virginia Tech, he called up Smart to discuss some candidates. (After the 2012 season, Virginia Tech actually made a run at Bobo, sending a plane to Athens, but

Georgia managed to keep Bobo by offering a three-year contract. The plane returned to Blacksburg without Bobo.)

The network of young coaches stayed in touch, and Beamer interviewed at Alabama when Saban was first hired. Nothing came out of it, but over the years, Smart kept Beamer on his radar, and the timing ended up working out. Beamer had some chances at other programs, but with Smart taking over at Georgia, that called to Beamer, who not only wanted to work with his friend, but also had always thought of Georgia as a premier destination and of Athens as a great place to live. This would mean going from working with two legends—Steve Spurrier and then his father Frank—to working for a first-time head coach his own age. But getting to know Smart over the years, Beamer was optimistic. "I thought he'd be dynamic at it," Beamer said. "Having grown up in the state of Georgia and been at Alabama when they had success, but then also just knowing him personally and knowing what kind of football coach he is, knowing what kind of recruiter he is, and just knowing his personality, he's definitely intense and demanding and competitive. You knew all that, but then there's also a side to him that you would see outside of football that I would see each summer as well. So I thought he'd be great going into it, and that was part of the desire and aspirations I had to work at Georgia and to work for him."

Chaney and Sam Pittman were the only announced staff hires between Smart's hire and Alabama's semifinal playoff game. Tucker and Schumann were going to be hired, but those were on hold until Alabama's season was over. That still left five positions for Smart to hire, and he ended up doing an interview-palooza at an awkward place: Georgia's team hotel in Jacksonville, where it was getting ready for the Gator Bowl.

It led to one of the more comical experiences I've witnessed as a beat writer and also showed the lengths that Smart went to keep things secret. Things were a bit weird in general. Coached by essentially the outgoing staff, the team still had a game to play. There were seniors on the team, who were never going to play for Smart. But there was Smart at the team hotel, sneaking around with Chaney while he interviewed people. The interviews were held on the ground floor in a hidden conference room—but not quite hidden enough.

When Smart and Chaney arrived at the team hotel on January 1, the day between Alabama's semifinal and Georgia's bowl game, the pair tried to sneak in through a side entrance to the hidden conference room. In the lobby at the time, I happened to be working on a story and saw Georgia's new head coach and offensive coordinator heading into the conference room.

Well, this was a chance for a scoop obviously. I texted my colleague on the beat at the time, Chip Towers, who came downstairs as we aimed for an exclusive. What we actually got was a comically long stakeout. There were two doors to the conference room, or at least we thought there were two doors. Chip took the one on the left, and I took the one on the right, the one I'd seen Smart and Chaney enter. As I was standing there, a third man, a dapper man with slicked-back hair and sunglasses, walked in. One thing I'm very good at is facial recognition, and knowing that Coley had been mentioned for Smart's new staff, I did a Google image search on Coley and surmised that was who had just gone into interview with Smart and Chaney. So now Chip and I realized it wouldn't be a quick stakeout.

It ended up being about six hours. Day turned to night, and we got so hungry we ordered food. But we didn't budge. We texted Smart, who did not respond. And as the hours went on, we began to wonder if there was a backdoor. And eventually, through the avenues that reporters have, we were assured that Smart, Chaney, and Coley were no longer in that room. Somehow they had escaped, we were assured. "Do we believe that?" Chip asked me.

"I don't think we have a choice," I said.

So we gave up. Smart had bested us. I filed a quick story just saying that Smart and Chaney had met with someone who looked a lot like Coley at the team hotel. It was something but not very much for a six-hour stakeout—six hours of my life I'll never get back.

Sighing deeply, I ordered some cake to go and walked back to my room in a building on the other end of the resort. As I approached the parking lot in front of my building, I noticed a couple men standing on the sidewalk, talking to each other. One of them looked familiar. It couldn't be, but it was…Kirby Smart.

After staking him out for six hours and then eluding us, here he was out in the open. So I approached him and stuck out my hand. "Did you get our texts?" I asked.

"Yeah, I got your texts," Smart said, grinning. "But if you respond to one person and not others, then that's not fair to the others."

"Was that James Coley who went in that conference room?" I asked.

"Well, I don't know if it was James Coley or not," Smart said mischievously before changing the subject.

We went back and forth a few more minutes, as the other man, who I didn't recognize and haven't seen around since, stood a few feet away. Smart mentioned something about recruiting. "I'd say last night [when Smart's Alabama defense had shut out Michigan State] was pretty good for recruiting," I told Smart.

"Yeah, but it was for the wrong team!" Smart said, with a smile.

We shook hands a short time later and parted, and when I got to the room I called Chip. "Guess who I just ran into?"

It would not be the last time Smart would frustrate the Georgia beat corps, who would not stop trying to sniff out what was going on. It became a game between us. He kept things clamped up more than his predecessor, and the media had to work harder for scoops. But when we did get something, Smart wouldn't get angry. He understood the game.

* * *

Kirby Smart finished his interviews in Jacksonville the next day with Shane Beamer, who interviewed first with Smart and Jim Chaney. When Smart left to go to the game, where he would do an in-game television interview, Chaney and Beamer chatted. Then they headed for the Jacksonville airport, where they met Smart and flew out together. The plane dropped Smart off in Tuscaloosa, Alabama, and then dropped Beamer off in Georgia. It was time to get to work.

By the time Alabama had won the national championship, the staff was basically in place. Smart hadn't hit on everybody he wanted, but it would still prove to be the right staff for the right time. It featured a great blend of experience and rising stars, a group that would largely be together through a very eventful first two years. Addressing the Macon Touchdown Club that spring, Mike Cavan heaped praise on what the head coach he had helped hire had done in assembling this group of coaches. "You've got the best staff I've seen at Georgia in a long time," Cavan said. "There is more excitement there than I've seen. I've been there a long time. I played on a championship team in the '60s, I coached in the '70s, I coached on a national championship in the '80s, three more SEC championships in the '80s. And I'll promise you: I've never seen the excitement like it is right now at the University of Georgia with our fans and with our players. Our coaches that are there with him are doing a great job with those guys. And you will be pleased next year when we kick it off."

But when addressing the same club, Smart put an emphasis on something else. He called it a "first-class, really competitive" staff and pointed to their SEC experience. Then he got into what he really wanted. "A lot of coaches have coached in the SEC," he said. "They have SEC experience. There is no greater challenge, let me tell you, than to recruit in the SEC. You bring yourself into the state of Georgia or the state of Florida and you go recruit. Every single school in the country will be in Georgia to recruit. Every big-time school will fly into Georgia to compete for a kid, and it's competitive. It's tough. It's a war out there. You better have guys ready to go to war and compete and be able to sell your program and what you have to offer."

Yes, recruiting was going to be paramount. And the biggest change that Smart was planning was the direct opposite of the narrative that arrived with him. Mark Richt had been criticized for letting too many Georgia recruits go elsewhere. Smart was a Georgia native who for the last nine years had pulled some of those very same Georgia recruits to Alabama like Reuben Foster, Alvin Kamara, and Geno Smith. And there were a couple recruits who were committed to Alabama at the time of Smart's hiring: a receiver named Tyler Simmons and a quarterback named Jake Fromm.

The clamor among Georgia's fans and administration was to keep those recruits home and that Smart would do so. The state was so rich in talent that merely by keeping the Georgia boys home it would make the program better. But Smart knew better. He came to Athens with a different plan.

The fact of the matter was that under Richt, Georgia had actually targeted in-state recruits sometimes to the detriment of out-of-state recruiting. The stated desire was to get the best players in Georgia and then reach outside the state for even better ones like Todd Gurley, Aaron Murray, A.J. Green, Matt Stafford, and Knowshon Moreno. They were all elite out-of-state players Richt had signed. (Those were also all offensive players.) "Under Richt, right or wrong, he was heavily based recruiting the state of Georgia," said Rusty Mansell, the longtime recruiting analyst for 247Sports and then Dawgs247. "He would sprinkle in a Matt Stafford or Knowshon Moreno or an A.J. Green, who were all great players. But it seemed like Richt would take his chances more on an in-state kid."

But Smart was going to go with a philosophy of, as Mansell put it: "We're going to trust our board more." They would make their recruiting board without as much regard to location of the players as to the talent level. So if the No. 1 recruit at cornerback happened to be from south Florida, and going after him meant forsaking a lesser recruit from Georgia, then the staff would do that. That was trusting your board. "It's not really a right or a wrong," Mansell said. "It's a philosophy."

That was very much an Alabama philosophy, which was borne of necessity. Alabama didn't have the luxury of all those recruits that Georgia had in state, and Alabama had to battle Auburn for those that were in its backyard. So the Crimson Tide went far and wide under Saban—whether that meant reaching across the border to Georgia or as far away as Hawaii.

There was another change Smart made to Georgia's recruiting philosophy. The list of recruiting targets would not only be more national, but it also would have more names on it. "More is better," Beamer said. Georgia was going to amass an army of recruiting staffers because it was going to amass a list of prospects that was pretty long. "A lot of coaches, that recruiting board, there's going to be very few names on there," Beamer said. "Their philosophy is: Okay, we're not going to have a lot of guys that we're recruiting. We're going to have a very select few. Whereas with Kirby..."

It was not a select few. Georgia was going to have a wide list of targets, was going to offer more players, and that was only after evaluating an even longer list of high school players. This combined the twin strategies of recruiting nationally and having a big board. Georgia had actually borne the fruits of that strategy a bit late in Richt's tenure, thanks to Jeremy Pruitt, who brought in a cornerback from Miami named Deandre Baker, who would go on to be an All-American and NFL first-round draft pick. In yet another instance of picking up where Pruitt's influence had laid the groundwork, Smart would follow that road map in recruiting.

That's where the staff would help. Offensive line coach Sam Pittman had worked all over the Southeast and Midwest and had contacts everywhere. Receivers coach James Coley was from Miami and known all around there. Beamer, the tight ends coach and special teams coordinator, had worked at Virginia Tech, South Carolina, and Mississippi State and seemed to know everyone in the country. Throw in running backs coach Dell McGee's contacts in Georgia, along with Smart's own contacts in his home state, and the staff felt well-positioned to prowl not only its own backyard, but also those of other schools.

They would build their recruiting board and then go after the best players period. When Smart spoke to fans in Macon, Georgia, that first spring, a fan rose and asked him: "Why do we turn on the television every Saturday and see all these boys from Georgia on other teams? Why don't we keep them home?"

This was the chance for Smart to issue a crowd-pleasing line about all that changing and keeping the boys home. Smart paused a moment. "You gonna give me extra scholarships?" He said.

That was Smart alluding to the NCAA limit of 85 scholarships —not to mention the yearly limit of 25 signees. But then Smart went into a long explanation of what he and his staff did at Alabama in researching just how many prospects came out of Georgia. "Did you know if you look at the first string and second string of every SEC school—we did this study at Alabama—and then we rank the states [they're from], Georgia's No. 1?" Smart said. "So everybody is coming in to come get players."

That was the twin message: We can't get everybody. And we'll have plenty of competition. Smart didn't want to say this publicly, but the plan, though not to sign everybody in Georgia, was to get the players they wanted, and there was a player there that night in Macon that he wanted.

As Smart spoke that night, there were a group of players below him being honored by the touchdown club. Two of them had signed with Georgia the previous month and would be in Athens that fall: defensive linemen David Marshall and Michail Carter. Two were in the next class and being targeted by Georgia: linebacker Nate McBride (who signed with Georgia) and defensive lineman Aubrey

Solomon (who spurned Georgia and went to Michigan before transferring to play for Pruitt at Tennessee).

The starting quarterback at nearby Houston County High School in Georgia also was being honored. When Fromm was given his award, the announcer mentioned to the crowd that Fromm was "verbally committed to the University of Alabama." There were groans in the audience. Fromm smiled. Smart had no reaction and just remained stone-faced. He knew the wheels were in motion to reverse that.

5

—

Changing the Culture

THE ANNOUNCEMENT CAME AT HALFTIME OF A GEORGIA basketball game, an otherwise unmemorable late January game against Arkansas. The crowd may have been a bit bigger because they were told that the new football coach would be speaking at halftime. But a spontaneous goose-bump moment happened before that. During a television timeout, out of a tunnel emerged Kirby Smart, who escorted a throng of recruits behind him. They walked procession-style almost the length of the court to the section of the bleachers, in which they would sit.

The crowd reaction was instantaneous. There was no slight murmur leading to an ovation. Almost as soon as they emerged into view, it began as an ovation. Fans stood and cheered. Maybe some were cheering for Smart. Maybe some were cheering for the recruits. Maybe some were doing both. Either way, it was a very public moment of buy-in and excitement from a fanbase that had privately been divided over the coaching change. Whatever people thought privately, the decision was made, and here was Smart, and they were cheering him lustfully. After about a minute, they sat down as the game resumed.

Then came halftime, and when Smart approached the scorer's table to get the microphone, almost every eye was on him. Students and fans alike raised their cell phones to take videos. The cheering resumed as Smart, who wore a pink polo, black suit jacket, and no tie, had his first chance to address Georgia fans in a crowd setting. "Thank you, guys. First off, let me tell you what an honor it is to be back home," Smart said, emphasizing the word "home." "All this passion and energy, we expect to see the same passion and energy come the spring game." Then came the Hail Mary. "We want 93,000 fans to come out to that spring game and support us. The easiest thing in recruiting is when everybody is uniting and pulling in the same direction. That's what we need, that's what we want, that's what we expect to get that done."

Smart didn't emphasize the 93,000 part. It just seemed a perfunctory thing, something someone would say but not expect. And he went on, giving a sort of state-of-things update to the crowd. "We're also recruiting right now with a lot of great guys we're pursuing, trying to finish off an awesome recruiting class to bring to Athens," he said. "Our current players are working here with Coach Sinclair and the new weight staff, our strength staff, and they're busting their tails to build what we want to build here, which is a championship football program."

That was it. Smart's speech lasted maybe a minute. But as soon as it was over media members and fans with social media accounts were blasting out a variation of "Kirby Smart wants to sell out the spring game." And away things went.

93K Day was born.

This was a marketing move and a calculated move made for recruiting. Georgia would be bringing in as many elite recruits as it could for the spring game, and this was an effort to sway them with something ambitious and different. Everybody has nice dorms, charismatic coaches, good facilities (arguable in Georgia's case at this point), tradition, and so on. This was an opportunity for something no one else had.

Plenty were skeptical. The game was free of charge, but would they really be able to draw that many? Privately, even those close to the team thought it would be more in the range of 70,000. It ended up exceeding everyone's expectations. There were not only about 93,000 in the stands, but there were also a few thousand watching from the bridge. There would be two things people would remember about that 2016 spring game: Jacob Eason, the true freshman and savior of the team, lit it up, and 93,000 showed up.

This was all a public demonstration of the excitement from the fanbase. Behind the scenes something arguably more important was happening: the changing of the culture. It would not happen quickly. "Not that anything was completely broken here before," said Smart guardedly at a news conference in January because he didn't want it to be perceived as criticizing a predecessor he liked and admired. "But this culture has to be set by Coach Smart and Coach Smart's staff, and we're doing that right now."

That spring and summer proved to be critical, though the dividends didn't show up until much later. But the groundwork had been laid for what was to come. Kevin Sherrer was connected to both Jeremy Pruitt and Smart. From his perspective this was a four-year process for Georgia to get here. There were necessary changes implemented the first two years with Pruitt's influence, and then they accelerated when Smart took over. "We all come from the same background. You could see a little bit of the change. But when Kirby got here, you really could see the change," Sherrer said. "And to me in any transition, there's always going to be a feeling-each-other-out type thing."

That was echoed by defensive back Aaron Davis, who saw the program for one year without Pruitt, two years with Pruitt, and then the first two years under Smart. "When Pruitt got there, he kind of brought over that Alabama philosophy that they had over there. They were winning a lot over there. So he had things to add as far as approaching the game mentally and the things that involved that," Davis said. "And when Coach Smart came over, he built even more on top of that and brought in the things that he used to do that were independent of Coach Richt, Coach Saban. I think it was a process that happened throughout the years. That's what I'd say."

But perhaps the biggest part of the culture change, and the underrated hero in Georgia's ascent to national power, was Scott Sinclair.

Those in the football industry vow that the most important staffer a head coach hires is the strength and conditioning coach. The image the average person may have of that coach is someone standing over a player and yelling at them as they do bench presses. That's a small slice of it. The strength and conditioning coach and his staff of four assistants oversee the players in the offseason, when there's no practices or games. They see the players more than the on-field football coaches do. The strength coaches are the ones who truly set the tone for the program throughout the year.

And that's even more vitally important for a new head coach. Smart was introduced in early December but didn't actually hold any practices until mid-March. It was his strength and conditioning staff that was allowed to meet and work with players in the weight room and essentially set the tone that Smart wanted for the program.

George O'Leary, the former Georgia Tech coach, had called Smart to recommend Sinclair. "You will not hire a better guy than him," O'Leary told Smart, per Smart's recollection.

Then at Central Florida, O'Leary knew Sinclair because he had been the assistant strength coach under him at UCF. O'Leary also wanted to recommend Ed Ellis, who had been his head strength coach. (When all three were at UCF, there was an ugly tragedy where a player died after a workout. It led to a court case, in which Ellis testified, but UCF's strength and conditioning staff was not implicated. The coaching staff, including O'Leary, was the focus of much of the case.)

In a world where connections are paramount, Smart didn't have any obvious ones with Sinclair. They had never worked together. A native of North Carolina, Sinclair had moved on to be the strength coach at Marshall after nine years as the assistant strength coach at UCF. There were other connections. Shane Beamer knew Sinclair and Ellis because they were all at Georgia Tech in 2005. And when Beamer was at Mississippi State a few years later, the starting long snapper was Aaron Feld, who would later become a cult hero on Georgia's strength staff under Smart. Still, it wasn't Beamer who suggested Sinclair. In a sign of how tight a ship Smart was planning to run, the two didn't even know they were both in the mix for jobs. The day before Beamer headed to Jacksonville to interview, he got a text from Sinclair. "Are you in Jacksonville?" Sinclair asked.

Beamer didn't know what to say because he was trying to keep it quiet. So he just replied "no," which was true because he wasn't there yet. "Are you?" Beamer texted back.

In another indication he knew how to be careful—something Smart surely appreciated—Sinclair didn't write back.

But eventually when Sinclair was hired, bringing Ellis and Feld with him, it was another good sign for Beamer, who had been around plenty of staffs despite his youth and knew how important a good strength staff would be to a new staff overall. "I thought they would be great once they got in there," Beamer said.

Smart was impressed right away, telling people that spring that he liked Sinclair's straightforward approach: "He's not a big rah-rah guy, a cheerleader guy like a lot of strength coaches. He's matter-of-fact, disciplined, believes in everything he does."

Sinclair also had a master's degree in strength training, which Smart liked. But since Sinclair and company hadn't worked with Smart before, there was a feeling-out period. "The hardest thing for Scott early on: Kirby had been around Alabama for so long and had seen how their strength and conditioning staff did things that early on. I think it was very much: 'I've seen this, this is how it works' and maybe didn't always mesh exactly with what Scott's plans were," Beamer said. "Then as time went on, Kirby developed more and more confidence and faith in Scott to where now it's his show, and they're doing what they feel like is best together."

Sinclair had the typical look of a strength coach. His head was shaved bald, he was short (about 5'10") but muscle-toned, and he had a bit of a scowl on his face. But his manner was much more positive. He could even be playful, eventually instituting a "Throwdown Thursday," in which the staff would record a fun video and send it out on social media. Sinclair and the staff also tried to keep things fun and interesting, matching players up against each other—or staffers—to cap off workouts. Sinclair and his staff also were pushing their new players, but they weren't doing it in an overbearing way. Sinclair had a good feel for people, and that showed up right away in his relationship with Georgia players. "It was just a fun time," Davis said. "The competition really helped us, too. We would always compete after our workouts. When you're dog tired, you just want to go get a protein shake and lay down. [But] we still had to compete at the end of our workouts. I just think he did a good job of pushing us and motivating us and also making sure he evaluated the guys and tried to see who was struggling, who needed to be picked up, who's excelling, and they need to be pushed to pick up somebody who is struggling. I think he did a good job of identifying that and then just riding off that to where we got to the point where guys could almost control the workout themselves, and he would just be the person who was facilitating it all."

Davin Bellamy put it more succinctly: "Some of the workouts were just like...my God. Just inhumane."

But it was instilling another core philosophy of getting comfortable being uncomfortable. Sinclair and his staff were trying to put the players in uncomfortable situations in the weight room, pushing their bodies to the limits before spring practice even began. It was setting the tone for the other core philosophy of making practices harder than games. That would become a mantra for the next two years and the secret to Georgia's success eventually.

Among those scarred by the previous year's experience with a new strength coach, Jeb Blazevich initially heard the same things from Sinclair as he had from Coach Hocke about revitalization, testing you, and gut checks. "And at this point, I just had two gut checks back to back," Blazevich said. "I'm sick of this. At what point can you just trust us?"

But Blazevich bought in to Sinclair, Ellis, and company fairly quickly because they clearly knew what they were doing. "They're not just hype men. They have a passion for what they're doing and they're knowledgeable," Blazevich said. "That's when it was okay, like gut check me. I'm willing to go through this and I think it was that first buy-in that first winter that really started to steer this ship the right way."

Jonathan Ledbetter characterized the one-year Hocke era more charitably but more damning with faint praise. "He was a good strength coach and he was young. He kind of did the basics of it. There's nothing wrong with that. It didn't necessarily get the job done. But we were strong. We were fast," Ledbetter said. "But when it came to the more important parts of football, which people say it's literally 90 percent mental and 10 percent skill, I'm a firm believer in that now just because of the transition we went through when Coach Smart came in. The whole idea was change the culture."

Sinclair, Ellis, Feld, and the strength staff helped things in a more cerebral sense. The team now had what were called "mind-set meetings," which were aimed at preparing the players to push themselves further in the weight room while being confident about it. The physical part of weight room training didn't change that much. At least, there wasn't any reinventing of the wheel when it came to running and lifting. It was the brain they were molding by incorporating trust exercises, telling players to say out loud what they wanted as they exercised, emphasizing positive over negative thoughts. "They showed us how to be mental beasts," Ledbetetter said. "Guys weren't ready to mentally train their minds, to be ready to attack situations. And we started tapping into that mental part of the game more than just the physical. You can play football, you can have a game, but if you don't have a team that's around each other, believing in each other, believing in the cause they're working toward, then it's not going to happen because you don't have goals and you don't have intentions based on those goals. And that's what they instilled in us once they got there."

Ledbetter, who often talks like he's leading a seminar, painted a picture of Sinclair and his staff that's the opposite of the stereotypical burly man, Neanderthal strength staff. It was a thinking man's staff. "They tapped into your emotional and spiritual essence of football," Ledbetter said. "And then that made us perform to a whole other level. That's what people saw when we went on the field, and the culture really started changing."

Prohibited by rule from overseeing the workouts, the Georgia coaches almost immediately began getting positive feedback from players on the strength staff. "I can vividly remember talking to guys that told me point blank—and I don't mean to knock anybody on the previous staff; I don't know those guys—but guys on the 2016 team told me there were games in 2015 where they literally walked on the field and felt physically overmatched to begin with at the point of attack just because they weren't strong because of how much running they did and all that," Beamer said. "I'm not a strength coach and I don't pretend to know what's right and what's wrong in terms of how they do things. But it is alarming when players, older players on the team, are telling you going into the 2016 season that for the first time in their careers they feel physically strong. That was an eye-opener for sure and a testament to Scott for the program he implemented."

Looking back a few years later, Davis summed it up this way: "Coach Sinclair really brought out the best of us in the weight room. He did a phenomenal job bringing in something new that I don't think any of us had seen before. That was one of the biggest changes as far as our day to day. You spend maybe eight months out of the year just training and you only spend three months playing in the game. So you spend way more time in the weight room in the offseason than on the football field."

The new coaching staff also provided a fresh jolt in the locker room. Players had felt stagnated with the same routine, but now under Smart "every day was different," Bellamy said. The Alabama Way was different. Pruitt had begun bringing that over, and Smart was completing the transformation. "When Richt was there, it was, 'We're going to take care of you. You're going to get the work in, but we're going to take care of you,'" Bellamy said. "But with [the Alabama people] it was: 'No, in order to be physical on Saturday, you have to be physical from Monday through Thursday. You've got to be physical all spring. You've got to be physical all camp.'"

There was also an emphasis on fighting through the pain. Pruitt had been disgusted with players tapping out during preseason practice in 2014. It may have taken awhile to take hold, but by Smart's first year, there were fewer players tapping out. The motto was that there was a difference between being hurt and being injured. If it was the latter, then you're out. But if you're only hurt, fight through it.

This was where Smart being able to flash his championship rings—not literally or even verbally, but everyone knew he had been there at Alabama—paid off. "Everybody wanted to talk about, 'All right Kirby's coming from Alabama, Georgia's doing everything that Alabama does,'" said Beamer, recalling that first year of off-field work. "But our players and our staff knew that it worked. What Alabama was doing worked in recruiting, it worked on the field, they won championships, and that's what we were hungry to do at Georgia. So Kirby's able to tell the players: 'Yeah, you're tired, yeah, practice is harder than maybe what you're used to, yes we're in pads multiple days a week, but this is what we did for however many years he was at Alabama. This is what we did. They're doing this exact same thing right now [in Tuscaloosa].' It was hard for guys to argue with that."

But not everyone was buying in. There was backlash. Not everyone took to the different style of their head coach right away. As intense as Pruitt had been, Smart was even more so.

71

"Pruitt was here," Bellamy said, putting one hand at a certain point in the air. "I'm talking about intensity level just crazy as shit. He was here." Then Bellamy put his other hand a few inches below. "Richt was here," he said. Then he moved his hand to well above Pruitt's level. "Kirby Smart was up here," he said.

That ran contrary to the image of Pruitt and Smart both being intense but Smart having the nicer touch. Bellamy grinned at that notion. "Maybe Pruitt would have been just like that if he had been the head coach," Bellamy said. "But you've got to realize he came in to be the defensive coordinator. There's still somebody over him in Richt. He was crazy as hell, but he wasn't trying to change the whole program. He wasn't the head coach. But when Smart got there, it was: I'm going to change this whole program."

That wasn't always well received by players. There were veterans who were established and had become comfortable. That was a mantra during Smart's first year: get comfortable being uncomfortable. Players who felt they had earned some credibility were not being given it. "Kirby doesn't care about pissing you off," Bellamy said. "'I'm going to tell you what you need to hear. You may not like it. You may get pissed off. Oh well.'"

That's why there was that backlash, as Bellamy described it. Bellamy himself admitted that entire first year under Smart was uncomfortable. An observer of the psyche of athletes, Bellamy made an observation about Smart. "When I say 'crazy,' I mean good crazy, Kobe Bryant crazy, Michael Jordan crazy. That's what drives Kirby," he said. "And I feel him on that."

Davis told people that Mark Richt was like a Godfather figure, overseeing everything and strict in how he did his business. "It's masterful to watch how he's able to take command of the room, and keep things under control," Davis said. "Coach Smart seems to bring what is the newer trend of young and fiery coaches, who are adding a lot of energy to the room. So at practice he'd be a little more animated than Coach Richt was but great coaches on both sides."

Smart's hands-on approach was noticed by one seemingly lesser profile new corner: J.R. Reed, who had transferred in and was thus ineligible to play in 2016. Reed wasn't regarded as much of a prospect. He hardly played as a freshman at Tulsa, and his recruitment to Georgia was seen as simply a ploy by Georgia coaches to land his cousin, star high school recruit Deangelo Gibbs. "But he still pushed me. That was the first thing I noticed," Reed said a few years later. "I was redshirting. I literally couldn't play that year, and he was still pushing me really hard like I was going to play. So that was one of the first things I really noticed and something different I hadn't seen in a coach."

Bellamy summed it up a different way. "With Richt we thought we were working, but we really weren't working," Bellamy said. "We were working to be a nine-game winning team. But Smart taught us to be a 12-win, 13–2 team. You have to be crazy. You have to have a passion for it, really work hard."

Kevin Butler came on around this time, too. The legendary Georgia place-kicker, who went on to kick for the Chicago Bears on its great '85 Super Bowl team, had re-enrolled at UGA to get his degree. The resourceful Smart saw an opportunity. As a student Butler could be an on-field assistant coach and work with the kickers. Butler readily agreed to work again with the program. Of course, Butler had been around the program a lot anyway. His son, Drew, starred as punter for the team from 2008 to 2011, and Kevin worked as a radio analyst on team broadcasts. So he was well aware of how things were before. "The culture beforehand was being satisfied with a good effort, and that's not enough and nor is that acceptable anymore," Butler said a few years later. "The atmosphere now is constantly pushing yourself to be better and knowing that you can always get better, and I think that's really what defines college football now from being elite. They strive to really get better, and the structure and their processes are 10,000 times more focused than I've ever seen…What he set in motion [in 2016] is the same thing he has going now."

* * *

As Kirby Smart settled in to his job, he was also making sure to keep his own staff on edge. He had a calm and measured tone in the office. He wasn't prone to outbursts like his old boss, Nick Saban, who Smart once half-joked caused assistants to hold hands under the table during staff meetings. But it was clear to Smart's new Georgia staff that certain things were expected. For one thing there was no dawdling. When you were in the office, you were working, and Smart had ways of making sure that was the case. "The one thing about him is he's very, very demanding at all times, whether it's the middle of February and it's kind of 'a slower time' or whether it's in the middle of October," Shane Beamer said. "There wasn't a lot of time to sit around and socialize and what-not. The time was very regimented. Your structure during the day year-round in the office was very regimented. He set that tone. You were always doing something, you were always working on something, you were always trying to maximize every minute of every day. Does he walk up and down the halls and scream and yell like he does on the sideline during games? No, not necessarily. But by no means mistake that for a lack of intensity every day in the office because he certainly brought that every day he was in the building."

That was what Smart had seen from Saban and was bringing to Athens. Yes, he worked his staff hard, but they would know that their boss was working hard, too. That would minimize the grumbling and maximize the work ethic, though there wasn't much grumbling. Beamer said everyone understood where Smart was coming from. Although he had hired self-motivated coaches and trusted them, this was a pressure environment because this was a pressure job. They got that. The previous coaching staff had been axed because 10 wins a season—cause for celebration in most other places—wasn't good enough here anymore. And nobody was going to pat them on the back anymore for merely being good. "Kirby's very demanding, but my two years there certainly made me a better coach," Beamer said. "I'm a very structured, organized, detailed guy. I feel like I'm a hard-working guy. And if you're those things, you're going to enjoy working at Georgia. And I did...You may not always like what he says or how he says it, but when you look back on it, you're like, 'Daggone, he was right.' And about a lot of stuff. It certainly opened my eyes to things. He's constantly looking for ways to get better, to make himself better, ways to make you better as a coach, ways to make the team better. So he's constantly looking for that."

Smart was also relentless with his recruiting. He was obsessed with it. "He would tell you every day what an animal it is in the SEC," Beamer said. "And he knows. You're going against some other great recruiters in the SEC, and what a war it was. You knew that every day. And no one was going to out-work him when it comes to that."

Beamer described the expectations for each assistant as being three-pronged: help Georgia win games; develop your players on and off the field, including academically and socially; and recruit. "Just be a hellacious recruiter. Because everything with Kirby is recruiting 24-7," Beamer said.

That wasn't much of an exaggeration. And it wasn't just about recruiting new players. "He recruits players. He recruits coaches. He recruits GAs. Everybody has the same mind-set and mentality," Jonathan Ledbetter said.

Ledbetter said that mentality even applied to one of his best friends who was a camera guy for the team. "We didn't have that mind-set before. It's evident throughout the whole facility, through-out the whole program," Ledbetter said. "That's what Georgia needed. Coach Richt was a phenomenal man, and I love him to death."

Mark Richt came to Ledbetter's house and cooked steaks for the whole family. It's not that he was sitting on his hands as a recruiter. He was not lazy. And he took an even closer role with his players on campus—and when they left. Richt started the Paul Oliver Network, which was dedicated to helping former players find jobs after football and named after the former Georgia and NFL defensive back who shot himself after his career ended. No one questioned Richt's sincerity in wanting what was best for his players. "His main purpose was to raise good men," Ledbetter said.

But some people wanted more. Isaac Nauta told Ledbetter he personally told Richt: "You're a good man and you love this program, but I think you're more interested in making good men than winning football games."

That was a bit unfair. Richt did win two SEC championships, five SEC East titles, and about 75 percent of his games. But the perception was still there. And even some of his players, such as Ledbetter and Davin Bellamy, think Richt was ultimately happy with winning 10 games and teaching his players to be great men, and not every assistant was wired to lead the team to greatness. "It's hard when you're doing it alone," Ledbetter said of Richt. "You can't do anything alone. You can't win the national championship alone."

Something else emerged that spring about Georgia's new coach. Smart was cutthroat.

That was apparent right away when it came to transfers. A.J. Turman was a tailback who had zero carries his first two years. Before spring practice began in 2016, he could look at the tailback depth chart and see the writing on the wall. So he informed Smart of his decision to transfer. Smart gave him his release but with stipulations. Because Turman, a Florida native, had said he wanted to go home, he could only go transfer and receive a scholarship at a school in Florida, but it could not be Florida (because it was an SEC school) or Miami (because Smart wanted to send a message that players couldn't just go re-join Richt).

Turman went public with the news, and, though Smart initially defended the stipulations, the coach eventually relented. Turman actually did go to his native state; he chose Florida Atlantic despite not having the restrictions anymore. (He ended up switching to defense under eventual Florida Atlantic coach Lane Kiffin.) And the NCAA later changed its transfer rules so that coaches like Smart could no longer block players from transferring to certain schools. Still, the whole thing was instructive. While in many ways being a player's coach, Smart was also going to be tough. He was going to manage his roster.

It was also one of the first signs that power was moving at Georgia. During the Richt era, athletic director Greg McGarity had been full-throated in unison with his coach that "life is too short" and that players should be able to transfer elsewhere. McGarity echoed the sentiment when it came to other sports, including men's basketball. But when the Turman issue came to light, McGarity merely said that Smart had educated him on the "transfer culture" and thus the administration went along with the change. And when I mentioned what had been a transfer "policy," McGarity interrupted to say it was a "stance," a stance that had changed under Smart.

That might have rubbed some players wrong, but inside Georgia's locker room, there were plenty receptive to having a bit of an edge. "He is a cutthroat type of coach when he has to be," Ledbetter said. "But in life people are only as good as their results. And people only respond to the results, so why would you not be cutthroat? Why would you be lackadaisical and basically be pretty much fake and not get anything from that? He's not that person. He's going to tell you just how it is and how it's supposed to be and he wouldn't get on you or say anything to you if it wasn't for your benefit or for the team's benefit."

Richt would stop short of doing things that were cutthroat. He was lenient to players who wanted to transfer. He forgave assistants who couldn't reel in the big recruit, especially if they made up for it with their coaching.

Smart would not do that. Tracy Rocker was let go after his first year when Georgia struggled to recruit top defensive linemen, especially in-state talent like Derrick Brown. And as time went on, Smart continued to push his assistants on the recruiting front, holding job security over their head like the sword of Damacles but also rewarding them with raises when they did recruit well.

* * *

Not everything that offseason went swimmingly. That first spring also gave Kirby Smart and his new team a taste of what would be a logistical nightmare. Because the indoor facility was being built—an annoyance in itself to Smart, who was used to having one at Alabama—the team had to bus out to a makeshift practice field that was practically off-campus. That required walking to the busses, riding on them for about 10 minutes each way, and then getting off the busses and to the field, etc. It amounted to about 45 minutes to an hour lost each day, which may not seem like a lot, but for a head coach used to breaking down each day's plan down to the second and not letting a moment go to waste, it was trying. "There was a whole adjustment period with that and trying to facilitate that and weather issues," Aaron Davis said. "It almost seemed like every week in camp there was at least one thunderstorm that derailed us."

There were some subtle changes in practice, too, which pointed to the style of play. Jim Chaney was simplifying the offense while trying to install the smashmouth approach that Smart wanted. Defensive players noticed that they were doing more drills aimed at blockers who were pulling. Offensive linemen learned to pull block, and defensive players learned to block the pulling blockers.

There were also guest speakers. This also wasn't different from the Mark Richt era, but sometimes they were different speakers with different aims. The central aim was to back up the message Smart, Scott Sinclair, and the staff were trying to instill. Sinclair and

Ed Ellis suggested some themselves. Dr. Kevin Elko, a motivational speaker who specializes in goal setting and leadership, was among those brought in. "I don't know if it was a drastic culture change," Davis said. "It was more instilling confidence in guys going out there on the field and expecting to win match-ups, and understanding that when we don't win those matchups, those things are not okay, and we need to correct that."

Finally, there was the adjustment that Smart had to make to being the head coach, which meant office politics. Richt had battled it for years—or perhaps not battled it enough—when it came to Georgia's administration, which many saw as not "all in" on football. It was what Jeremy Pruitt had voiced when it came to the lack of an indoor facility. *If Georgia really cares about football, why don't they have an indoor facility?*

Well, one was coming now, and Smart privately had assurances that more was coming, including a much-needed new locker room and recruiting area at Sanford Stadium, which Richt had wanted, too. But more would be needed to be done as the years went on, and Smart knew that. Georgia was behind in facilities. More than a year into his tenure, Smart voiced that, saying the school was still playing "catch up" to a lot of the schools in the SEC West.

Georgia's administration, however, was finally seeing the light, and seeing that when football won, it brought in money in the way of ticket sales and donations. You need to spend money to make money, as the Alabamas and Auburns and LSUs of the world had learned years ago. And now that Georgia's administration had a head coach it was truly invested in, it would invest in him. Smart and his staff received more money for their recruiting budget than Richt had, and the administration generally said yes a lot more than it said no. Perhaps Smart had someone to thank in Jeremy Pruitt.

For all the purported problems Pruitt had caused, he had also planted the seeds for what Smart would benefit from. Pruitt had brought with him a seeming army of Alabama types, whether it was Kevin Sherrer or off-field analysts. But Smart, unlike Pruitt, was going to be very careful not to alienate his superiors—at least publicly. In private meetings with boosters, Smart often didn't hold back, citing the deficiency in facilities. This was a big reason Smart wanted—and the administration went along with it—to close many of these meetings from the public and media.

The donors were listening. This was where it went beyond just the excitement of a new coach. It was even beyond the respect they felt for someone who had been at Nick Saban's side and had won championships. For Georgia people this was one of their own. This was someone who had played there, grown up there, and felt the same pull that they did. There was something about knowing the terrain and bleeding the Red and Black. The buy-in of what Smart was selling was happening on and off the field. That spring and summer, the groundwork was being laid for what was to come.

6

A Good Start

T HIS WAS THE SWAN SONG YEAR FOR THE GEORGIA
Dome, a place where both Kirby Smart and the Georgia football program had experienced plenty of great and painful moments.
They were almost all great moments for Smart and oftentimes at
the expense of Georgia. When the 2012 SEC Championship Game
had ended abruptly, the confetti rained down on a devastated
Georgia football team, and Smart was among the first on the
field celebrating with his Alabama players. Afterward he and Mike
Bobo embraced outside the locker room. Smart had celebrated
four SEC championships in this building. Georgia had celebrated
two, but the last one was 10 years ago, and Mark Richt had finished 0–3 in the building, including blowout losses to LSU and
Boise State and that heartbreaking, excruciating loss to Alabama.
The building had become a symbol for where the program had
fallen short.

Now it was the site of the program's new era under Smart,
who was trying to bring karma with him after winning four SEC
championships on that field, including months before on the same
night he signed the paperwork to be Georgia's head coach.

There had been a couple other subplots heading into the game.
Jason Eason would not be starting. Smart and Jim Chaney went
with the veteran Greyson Lambert, but the plan was to put Eason
in the game at times and get his feet wet as they worked toward
eventually making him the full-time starter. The other big story,
the inspirational one, was the return of Nick Chubb, who less than
a year after a potentially career-ending knee injury was set to play
and perhaps play a lot. Against that backdrop the debut of the new
head coach was almost an afterthought as the team bus pulled into

the Georgia Dome, a place the players felt they would be visiting one more time that season in December.

Smart chose three captains for the game against North Carolina: Chubb (for obvious reasons); senior center Brandon Kublanow, who would be among the first holdovers to really buy in to the new coaching staff but would not be around to bear the ultimate fruits of it; and junior safety Dominick Sanders, who would leave a complicated legacy because of one fateful play. Georgia called heads. It was heads, and Kublanow informed the official Georgia would receive.

The first play of the Kirby Smart era was a North Carolina kickoff, a touchback. The first real play was a handoff to Chubb, who gained six yards. The Kirby Smart era had officially begun, as had the career of a new head coach, and the initial bumpiness would foreshadow larger ones to come. "It was really weird," Smart said afterwards, "a comedy of errors, flipping over the headphones, trying to figure out who I'm talking to because I didn't have to do that before."

Off the field it had been an eventful summer. Two situations showed both sides of Smart: the hard-nosed and cutthroat side, in which he showed no sentiment toward his old boss. Then there was also the softer side of Smart, exemplified in how he handled Jonathan Ledbetter.

Ledbetter was one of the many Georgia players who Smart knew well before he arrived because he had recruited him. In fact, Ledbetter, a defensive lineman originally from New York whose family had moved to the Atlanta area, committed to Alabama. But when Georgia and Jeremy Pruitt lured Ledbetter's older brother, Joseph, a tight end at a Division II school, to Georgia with a scholarship, it helped convince Jonathan to switch to Georgia. Ever cognizant that today's loss could be tomorrow's gain, Smart didn't hold it against Ledbetter.

Ledbetter was by all accounts an affable, approachable, and good kid. But he also ran into some trouble the summer before his sophomore season in 2016. Ledbetter was caught trying to enter a downtown Athens bar with a fake ID. That drew an arrest, which was eventually dismissed, but it was followed months later by a more serious incident. After a night out, he was then found by police asleep in his car at an intersection. The car was still running, and police could not wake up Ledbetter even after turning on the siren and blaring a horn. After blowing a breathalyzer above the legal limit, Ledbetter was charged with a DUI.

The two offenses meant a four-game suspension. Cynically, you could argue that Ledbetter was too good a player to simply be cast aside, and that's true. But Smart also took a central role in what followed. Ledbetter was sent to treatment and remained with the team over the course of the 2016 season while also continuing to undergo treatment. "He took a chance on me because he knew the kind of person I was and he knew the household I came from," Ledbetter said. "It goes deeper than, *Oh, I know this kid.* He knows everything about me. He recruited me and he took the time to know my family, know my background. And he knows that about everybody."

Ledbetter was a cerebral kid from New York. Smart was a football coach's son from small-town south Georgia. And yet they connected in a deep way. Part of that was their shared experiences. When Ledbetter was going through his struggles, Smart sat down with him and explained his own family background. Ledbetter didn't want to divulge it publicly but said that the two bonded over some specific things in common. "He told me what he had to go through when he was growing up, and I was like, 'Well, damn, that ain't easy either,'" Ledbetter said. "He understood where I was coming from and everything that was going on with me."

This may not have been what brought them together specifically, but Smart talks often about his older brother, Karl, going through cancer treatment when they were growing up and how hard it was for the family. Karl pulled through it, and every summer Kirby goes with the team to Camp Sunshine, the summer camp for kids and family members going through cancer treatment. Kirby attended the camp when he was young. Mark Richt regularly took Georgia players there, and Smart picked up the tradition. "I'm a firm believer in you're only as good as your adversities, you're only as good as your experiences," Ledbetter said. "People in life will just go through with the breeze. They're not able to go through the hard stuff like everyone. They'll crumble."

Over his final two seasons, Ledbetter became one of the leaders on the defense, the player credited with half the sack on Tua Tagovailoa in overtime of the national championship. (The one that set up the second-and-26 play.) A cynic would argue that a lesser player would be dispensed with by a coach and sent on to a junior college, a la Last Chance U. That may be true. Ledbetter cleaned himself up off the field, contributed to the team, and emerged as one of the team's best leaders and best citizens, crediting Smart in large for all that. "It's weird to have a coach who's just your friend," Ledbetter said in 2018, as his career was ending. "I couldn't be more thankful for Kirby Smart. Me and him have a lot of history. He's helped me out a lot in my life and helped me become the man I am today. He's opened my eyes to a lot of things in the real world and real life."

* * *

Maurice Smith was the first victory for Kirby Smart over Nick Saban. A senior defensive back who had started only two games for the Crimson Tide, Smith was a seemingly minor player. But these were not two coaches who overlooked anybody. Smith was capable of starting and at minimum being a solid contributor, and both Saban and Smart knew that. So did Mel Tucker, who had coached Smith in 2015. So when spring practice at Alabama ended and Smith, seeking some certainty of starting in his final year in college, decided to transfer, Georgia was a natural landing spot.

Smith was also graduating; so under NCAA rules, he could be eligible immediately.

There was one major problem. SEC rules stipulated that players could not transfer within the conference and be on scholarship. Smart and his parents, however, were undeterred. And rather than throwing up his arms and deferring to his old boss, Smart opted to fight. What ensued over many months was a dramatic, behind-the-scenes battle. Smith alleged that someone at Alabama ordered his locker trashed and threw away his stuff. He also alleged that he was banned from the football facility. "On Friday, June 17, I arrived at the athletic facility locker room to find my locker cleaned out and all of my personal belongings in the trash [photo attached]," Maurice Smith wrote in a letter to an appeal committee at Alabama. "These personal items included my family photos, written goals, inspirational and sentimental items memorializing my deceased former friend, roommate, and teammate, Altee Tenpenny, and items of personal value from my former teammates."

Saban had met with Smith and his mother, Samyra, on June 27 and told them that "Georgia was not an option." But he did say he could go to Miami, and initially Smith agreed. But a day later, Smith had a change of heart. He still wanted to pursue going to Georgia, where his old coaches were. But Alabama was not going to sign off.

The public didn't know about any of this until Samyra Smith went public. I had been tipped off that all this was happening and got in touch with Samyra, who provided all the details over the course of several days. It resulted in a sort of drip-drip-drip that exerted public pressure on Saban. At a press conference I also asked Smart about the situation, and he officially broke with Saban, confirming that he was recruiting Smith, which was all Smart could say under NCAA rules, while also issuing a policy statement: "Every young man that we want to bring here to the University of Georgia, we want them to graduate from this place. And if they have an opportunity to go to a graduate school at another place, I certainly think that that's something that we're going to let them do if they have an opportunity to go once they graduate," Smart said. "I think that's important to know."

Before the microphone could be handed to another reporter, I quickly followed up. So if a graduate transfer wanted to go anywhere else in the SEC, Smart would be fine with it?

"Absolutely," Smart said.

It was the reverse of a few months before when Smart had declined to let A.J. Turman transfer anywhere he wanted. This showed that Smart would do what it took—but with a distinction. Turman had not graduated and had not in his interpretation earned the right to go anywhere he wanted. Smith had graduated and thus earned it.

A few years later, Saban said the that the Maurice Smith situation caused him to lose sleep. Saban eventually relented, punting the issue to the SEC office, which was not going to stand in the way given the public sentiment. Smart had been worried that commissioner Greg Sankey, whose office was an hour away from Tuscaloosa, would not want to tick off Saban. But Sankey knew he had more than just one constituency, so he signed off on Smith's waiver, adding stipulations tied to Smith getting his master's degree at Georgia. Smart had won round one against his old boss.

Smart also won his first game as a head coach, but it required a comeback. North Carolina led 24–14 in the third quarter when Jacob Eason, playing off the bench, hit Isaiah McKenzie for a touchdown. Then Georgia's defense and Nick Chubb took over. Georgia forced a safety, and then Chubb put the game away with a 55-yard run with 3:34 left in the game. Incredibly, Chubb had not only returned to action, but also had 222 yards. Eason didn't start but had played most of the game. Brian Herrien, an unheralded tailback recruit, had incredibly scored a touchdown on the first play of his career. There were some warning signs of struggles to come, including that the offensive line gave up four sacks, three of them of poor Greyson Lambert. But all in all, it was a triumphant debut for the new era.

When the game ended, Smart took the stage with his team and showed his playful side, putting on a ceremonial leather helmet and mimicking a Heisman pose with Chubb, Sony Michel, and others. Smart and his players reveled in the victory. There was plenty of talk of trying to get back there in December, which seemed a very attainable goal, considering the state of the SEC East and how Georgia had played that night. Nobody on that Georgia team, as it turned out, would ever set foot in the Georgia Dome again, at least without a ticket.

The next week was supposed to be a week off essentially. The opponent was Nicholls State, a mere FCS team. It nearly ended up being a disaster. This was one of those dreaded noon starts, where the home fans arrive late or not at all, sapping the atmosphere, and the home team itself often isn't as amped for the game. But it was also the week after an emotional win. In retrospect, the letdown factor was obvious.

Eason had gotten his first college start. Smart and Jim Chaney decided the time had come to get him the experience he needed. The result was some rough moments, including an interception and a sack, and some rushed throws. Chubb also didn't have the huge holes he'd had the week before. The crowd was restless through a sluggish first half, which saw Georgia only lead by six. When Nicholls State took a one-point lead midway through the third quarter, groans of panic ensued.

Disaster appeared to be averted when Eason and McKenzie hooked up on a 66-yard touchdown, and then Lorenzo Carter returned a 24-yard fumble for a touchdown. But then Nicholls State put together two more scoring drives in the fourth quarter, and with only minutes left, Georgia clung to a 26–24 lead. Disaster appeared very possible.

Lambert came to the rescue. He had been inserted back in the game in the fourth quarter, and after two Chubb runs set up a third and 7, Georgia was pinned at its own 12. Lambert found

Michael Chigbu on the sideline for a nine-yard completion. First down. Georgia ran out the clock, and disaster was officially averted.

Smart didn't hold back after the game in the locker room or his postgame press conference. "It's important that we understand that our football team has to get better. It's frustrating," he said. "A lot of guys didn't execute, didn't play well, and that's my responsibility. We've got to improve because there are good teams down the road."

One was Missouri, where Georgia once again barely escaped the following week. Eason, starting again, faced fourth and 10 from Missouri's 20-yard line in the final minutes with Georgia trailing 27–21. Eason found McKenzie in the middle of the end zone, and McKenzie wrestled the ball away from a defender. Georgia's defense iced it by recovering a fumble near midfield in the final minute.

Smart was now 3–0. Georgia had trailed in all three games, and the competition had not been stellar, but he was still the first Georgia head coach since 1938 to start 3–0. Georgia players were getting to know their new coach's gameday style. He was intense and as hands-on as promised in that first press conference the previous December. Perhaps more so. "When I look at him, there's a connection because he really does feel like he's in the game," Aaron Davis said. "He really does feel heavily invested in it, and I think that's why he elicits a lot of the emotions from people like me on the sideline."

But people were learning that Smart had a way of turning the emotions on and off when appropriate. "Behind closed doors there is a different way of going about things," Davis said. "You're not going to be as fired up in the DB meeting room as you are on gameday."

Practices stood out to Loran Smith, the longtime Georgia athletics historian who had observed the team under Vine Dooley, Ray Goff, Jim Donnan, and Mark Richt, as well as plenty at other schools. "The intensity about practices," Smith said, "I mean…I get tired just walking where the ball is."

Smart and Mel Tucker played some good cop/bad cop with the defense. But Tucker wasn't afraid to rip people, too. From star players to walk-ons, they treated everyone the same. Maybe Roquan Smith wasn't yelled at much because he was Roquan Smith and tended to always do everything right. But other starters recalled getting screamed at when they erred. And during the viewing periods, even the media got a taste of Smart jumping on the walk-on scout teamers when they lined up in the wrong place. But that also meant giving a real shot to everyone. That happened under Mark Richt and Jeremy Pruitt, so it wasn't necessarily a mark of the new staff.

But there was definitely a sense of change. The program felt renewed, and with Eason settling in as the quarterback, optimism in the fanbase was rampant. As it turned out, though, before things got even better, they would get even worse.

7

A Rough Finish

T HE LOSING BEGAN ON A NICE MORNING IN OXFORD, Mississippi, a day that the team and its fanbase were sent crashing down to Earth. Ole Miss routed the Bulldogs by 31 points. That was one way to lose. The other side of the spectrum came a week later when Tennessee won on a Hail Mary on the final play of the game after Georgia thought it had won on its own incredible play: a Jacob Eason 47-yard strike to Riley Ridley with 10 seconds left.

In the locker room afterward, Kirby Smart addressed the team and chose his words carefully. He told the players "how much he hurt for them," as Loran Smith said later. He did not specifically call out Rico McGraw, the sophomore cornerback whose boneheaded penalty—running on the field to celebrate the Ridley touchdown— caused a 15-yard penalty and set up Tennessee's game-winning play. "Now I know he wore [McGraw's] ass out the next week, and he eventually left, and I'm sure he had something to do with it," Smith said.

As painful as the Tennessee game was, the Vanderbilt game was pitiful. Georgia's offense couldn't move the ball, managing only 16 points. The defense gave up a few big plays—enough for Vanderbilt to have a one-point lead. Even then Georgia still had a chance, but a fourth-and-inches call by Jim Chaney—giving the ball to Isaiah McKenzie in the backfield for a run to the sideline marker—was stopped just short.

Chaney later said it was clearly the wrong call. Looking back on the play call years later, Jonathan Ledbetter could only laugh. "A stretch play, the smallest guy on the team, we needed one yard," Ledbetter said. "Ideally, you would have given that to Nick Chubb, who averages 4.5 yards after contact. But it was stuff like that, that hurt, that made us hard and want more for our team and want more for each other and the program."

Something also struck me about how Smart handled the end of that Vanderbilt game. As the measurement made it official, Smart did not rant and rave or throw his headset. He simply grimaced and turned and pointed for his defense to get on the field. He was composed despite the realization that his team had lost at home to the frequent SEC cellar dwellers. So many things had gone wrong in that game from special teams (which allowed Vanderbilt a 90-yard return to start the game) to offense and defense.

There was so much to diagnose, and it was a noon game, so there was plenty of time remaining in the day for recriminations and panic. That didn't happen. "He has been the best I've seen at keeping the focus on whatever is next whether it's the next play, it's the next touchdown, it's the next score, it's the next game," Georgia sideline reporter Chuck Dowdle said. "But nothing beyond whatever is next. And that's what you focus on."

Life had to go on, especially recruiting. Shane Beamer, for instance, had a recruit in town for the weekend for an official visit. Beamer carried on as if it had been a win, as did the other coaches hosting recruits. Beamer went to dinner with the recruit and his family. Sunday morning the coaches had a post-mortem on Vanderbilt that Beamer remembered being all business. And then Sunday night, Beamer and the recruit went out to dinner again. "It wasn't like sitting around the dinner table, and everyone's feeling sorry for themselves," Beamer said. "You had to make sure this high school prospect had a great time."

Then Beamer boarded a plane Sunday night to go to Virginia to recruit. They had an off week, a bye week before playing archrival Florida. So Smart sent his staff out recruiting. One of the few acknowledgements Smart made to his coaches about the way the season was going was when it came to recruiting. He would tell his staff: "Guys, the only way we're going to get out of this is to recruit—and recruit great players."

Indeed, by the Vanderbilt game, it was clear this season was going nowhere, or at least not to the SEC Championship Game. When the Bulldogs went down to Jacksonville and were handled convincingly by Florida, it dropped their record to 4–4. They would pull together and win their next three only to lose at home to archrival Georgia Tech, blowing a fourth-quarter lead in the process. There was now snickering from national media and other types. It didn't help that Mark Richt had Miami in better shape. The optics weren't great.

But others pointed out that Alabama had also struggled in its first season under Nick Saban (and Smart), going 7–6 and losing at home to Louisiana-Monroe. On the drive back from the Florida game, Georgia fans could see a barn painted overnight that read: "TRUST THE PROCESS." That's what Smart and his staff were preaching. Smart's postgame speeches were peppered with phrases blending criticism and positive reinforcement: "That wasn't us... That's not who we are."

Smart also continued to be intense. He yelled a lot at practice. That made it a bit hard for players to gauge when it was just normal Smart or whether it was legitimately angry Smart. That was a challenge. But players also began to notice that their coach wasn't moody. "You weren't walking on egg shells wondering who you were gonna get," Jeb Blazevich said. "He was consistent in how he approached it. I'd rather somebody—even if he was the worst guy in the world or a jerk—I'd rather he be that every day than a nice guy some days and a horrible guy other days. I'd take consistency over anything. He was a passionate, knowledgeable, intense coach. And I appreciated him for it."

Still, holding everything together and avoiding a season, in which everyone mentally packed it in was going to be a challenge. The offense was struggling again. It didn't help to have a freshman quarterback and a smaller offensive line. But much like the previous year, the play-calling was coming into question. "On the offensive side, we didn't trust Chaney at all," Blazevich said. "He would do some things that seemed stubborn and prideful, and it was just more of the same. It was like: this was working; now let's try to air the ball out and prove that we could do it as opposed to why don't we just stick with what was working. So that's when the negativity creeped back in from some of the older leaders that year."

The Florida game was such a moment. Georgia fell behind, and Chaney got pass-happy. Eason threw it 33 times (completing less than half of his attempts and finishing with only 143 yards) while Chubb only got nine carries, and Sony Michel got three. It all pointed to a criticism of Chaney throughout his tenure. He was great at devising a gameplan, but when things went awry, the in-game adjustments weren't there. "If they're not performing well, I understand trying something else, but he'd always either stick with something too long or try to switch it up at a weird time," Blazevich said. "He was an amazing schemer, but I think he was terrible at in-game calling...I guess it was his competitiveness that came out just a little bit too much and not being willing to operate differently. That was the main gripe. We can't trust him. We all loved him. We see the plays he puts in every week."

And what helped Georgia over the next year and a half was that Chaney was not arrogant. He was the opposite. He lacked any ego, according to those who knew him for years. So after the debacle in Jacksonville, Chubb and Michel felt comfortable enough to talk to Chaney about why they weren't used enough. Chaney listened and welcomed the feedback, and things really did seem to change.

As for the defense, it was doing okay. In fact, looking back it was laying the groundwork for a really good season. The unit endured some growing pains but was finding the right personnel. Midway through the Ole Miss debacle, sophomore Deandre Baker was plugged in at cornerback. He never left the lineup again on the way to an All-American career. Other players were getting much-needed experience and playing well, such as J.R. Reed, the strong safety who was proving to be quite a surprise.

Special teams, however, was an adventure. And in general things weren't as in sync as they could be. Ledbetter thinks part of the problem was that too many veterans had only played under one style of coach, whether it was Richt or their position coach, and those were the ones who tended to set the tone in the locker room. There weren't a lot of seniors on that team, but there were just enough sprinkled throughout the team and the locker room for it to matter, at least a little bit. "It was kind of difficult to get them to buy in to the new thing because they had already seen something for so many years," Ledbetter said. "And the juniors, they were kind of tweeners."

Since those juniors had two years left or maybe just one if they went pro, they were feeling things out and not quite committing all in, though they eventually would. The coaching staff was still feeling its way through as well. "They didn't all mesh together. It wasn't everybody on the same mission, the same goal," Ledbetter said. "It wasn't selfishness. They just hadn't had time to feel each other out and read each other out and figure out how that dynamic works."

That included Smart and Chaney, who had never worked together. They each had different impulses that would sometimes clash. Smart wanted to be hands-on, and while Chaney generally was easygoing, sometimes there would be friction. Smart would pull back and let Chaney call plays and then wonder why runs weren't being called in the Florida game.

There were also the holdovers. Kevin Sherrer, the outside line-backers coach, was bred in The Alabama Way and had previously worked with Smart in Tuscaloosa, so that was less of an issue. Sherrer ended up leaving Athens to re-join Pruitt at Tennessee with a raise and promotion. Tracy Rocker, on the other hand, was fired after Smart's first year. His contract was not renewed after Georgia missed out on some key defensive line recruits. (Rocker also ended up on Pruitt's first staff at Tennessee after taking a year off coaching.) "Not to say they couldn't work together, but there were different ideals," Ledbetter said. "There was already a culture set in stone with Coach Richt that Kirby was trying to change, but you had coaches who had already been bred into that Mark Richt era, and it had to change. You had people butting heads over stuff that you really shouldn't have been butting heads over."

The chemistry in the locker room was fine but more subdued. Smart had assigned players to a leadership council to instill what the coaches wanted off the field. The seeds were being planted for later, but during this 2016 season, it wasn't playing out as an advantage. There was a leadership void because the best leaders were not the best players, and the best players were either not good leaders or not asserting themselves yet. "You can be an awesome guy, give your whole heart and soul to the team, but if you're not performing on the field, people don't want to hear from you," Blazevich said. "We had a lot of leadership, but there was just a void in terms of the star players being the leaders."

Some players thought the losses were the byproduct of the culture change—making practices harder than the games, overhauling the strength and conditioning program—which was taking root yet too early to show results. "That was something that was brewing up in 2016. It took everyone some time to get adjusted to it," Aaron Davis said. "But I still felt like even in 2016 we still had the pieces to go further than what we did. I think everyone would say that the 2016 season was a huge letdown for us. We still had great players there. We had the talent that matched up with everyone else. We just for some reason weren't executing the way we needed to."

Keep in mind, Smart had taken over a winning program. That means a different dynamic. When you take over a struggling program and try to make it better, it's often easier for a new coach to walk in and immediately improve the record, but the long-term results may not be better. Smart, on the other hand, was taking over a team coming off consecutive 10-win seasons. Winning wasn't the issue. Winning *more* was the issue. So there was an element of the old Bill Parcells adage of breaking things down before they could get better again and then even better: short-term pain for long-term gain. "You had a team who was halfway divided between the younger guys and the older guys who had seen it this way and lived like that way forever," Ledbetter said. "It just had to take its course. It's not going to be overnight, and we realized that it wasn't going to be like that. People had to just believe—not that the grass was greener on the other side—but there was a light at the end of the tunnel. You had to keep fighting through the hard stuff. We had some good games. Statistically, we played well. We just lost some games. And in some games, we got destroyed. We had to feel that we had to get all that out so we could become our better selves."

What Blazevich also noticed was another hallmark emerging: Smart wasn't changing the approach based on wins and losses. The conditioning plan wasn't changing. The strength plan wasn't changing. The approach at practices wasn't changing Sunday through Friday. "Just seeing that consistency, that was really refreshing," Blazevich said. "That was the thing that started to get us buying into the process. Things were still going wrong, same thing as last year. We're still not scoring points, we're still losing games we shouldn't lose, we're worse off from last year in the win-loss column…but we had consistency throughout it."

The view on the coaching staff was the same. There weren't any grand meetings about staying the course, according to Beamer. But there was a day-to-day sense that nobody needed to panic similar to how Saban's first year at Alabama had been treated inside the program even as outside criticism swirled. "Everybody talks about Alabama and the process and all that, but it's true, and that's the way that we did things at Georgia," Beamer said.

The win over Auburn in late November, knocking off the then-No. 9 Tigers, was a good reminder that the potential was there. But the reaction inside the coaching room to beating Auburn and losing to Vanderbilt was essentially the same. The coaches addressed what went well, what they needed to do better, and then moved on. "After a win there wasn't a lot of coming in there on Sunday morning and patting everyone on the back and telling them how great they are. And it was the same thing when we met with the players on Monday," Beamer said. "And when we lost, it wasn't coming in there and ripping people's butts and going off on an emotional tangent. It was very consistent. Every day you knew what to expect, and that was 365 days a year. And that carried right into the season. It was just a consistent [sense] of we're on this journey, and every single day, we know what the plan is."

As the losses piled up, Smart's treatment of the media was also coming into view. It had already been frosty during the first nine months of his tenure. Smart immediately "Saban-ized" the program by making assistant coaches and freshmen off limits (save for the offensive and defensive coordinator for one day in August) and also generally limited player availability. This was a drastic change for not only the media, but also UGA's sports communications department, which was renowned nationally for its work with the media. Claude Felton, who had been with the team since the 1970s, oversaw a staff that was almost a yearly "Super 11" winner of the Football Writers Association of America for its work with the media. After Smart's arrival the Super 11 awards petered out for Georgia through no real fault of Felton or his staff.

Smart also began to adopt the persona of his mentor at press conferences. Just like Saban, Smart was liable to jump on a reporter who asked a question he didn't like. He did not suffer fools. It made several longtime people around UGA's administration wince, and some debated whether to go to Smart and say something along the lines of, "Hey, we don't do that here."

But Saban's press conference persona was by design. Smart knew that and was following that model, too. When the coaches were facing the cameras, they saw it not really as answering the public's questions but as sending a message to their team. That was the main focus. For example, Saban once jumped down the throat of my friend, Gentry Estes, who had just started covering Alabama at the time, about something seemingly mundane: whether he was worried about the team's focus that week. Following the press conference, Saban sent for Estes, who came to Saban's office, where he was having a salad, and Saban explained that he understood the question, but that he had to answer the way he did in order to make sure his team knew that focus should *not* be an issue that week.

There would be moments like that for Smart as well. Over the next few years, he often acted one way when the cameras were on—stern, glaring, and chippy—and then more relaxed once they were off. There would also be times Smart obviously felt bad about the way he handled a situation—enough so to make sure that a beat writer who was the object of a press conference tirade was leaked a scoop.

Smart may not have been publicly nice with the media, but he was informative. If you asked a question, he would answer it even if you didn't like the answer. And while he strictly limited the length of his press conferences—generally 20 minutes for the big weekly presser and 12 for the weekly post-practice presser—Smart talked so fast that he crammed a lot in that time. He also wasn't afraid to criticize his players, as people like Terry Godwin and Richard LeCounte found out.

Chuck Dowdle, who interviewed the coach after games, also came away with more information than he was used to getting. "He's been a pleasure to deal with after games," Dowdle said, "because he will tell you stuff, answer questions. He doesn't try to gloss over anything. He's real point blank about, 'We didn't do this well, we can't do that, we've got to be better at this or better at that.'

I just find that he will answer a question if you will ask a question. And Coach Richt—and I love Mark—a lot of times he didn't want to answer questions. Kirby will answer questions."

Smart also didn't play favorites or suck up to people. He would push back on CBS or ESPN experts during their private meetings before games. Gary Danielson, the CBS color analyst, didn't have a problem with that. "He's competitive even in our meeting rooms. And if you asked him a sideways question, he'd let you know," Danielson said. "And I'm fine with that. But he answers the questions. He doesn't always like the question. But he answers them, and sometimes he'll just say: 'That's none of your business. That's something I don't talk about.' Which I like to hear. You're probably the same way. I'd rather have somebody go: 'That's somewhere I don't want to go' rather than lying to me."

The logistical annoyances of that season were also playing out. The team was still bussing to practice every day, losing valuable minutes by doing so. They were forced to practice outside in the heat or lose practice altogether when it rained. The NCAA's 20-hour rule, which limited players to only 20 hours per week of football activity, loomed. "When transportation is included within our 20 hours a week, we had to get to practice as quickly as possible and try to leave right on time. And when we're there, it's a tremendous amount of pressure to make the most out of practice," Davis said.

Looking back a few years later, Ledbetter outlined the weekly practice grind. "You've got 15, 16 period, two-hour and 20-minute practices, full pads, four times out of the week sometimes and you've just got to trust your coaches sometimes," he said. "Of course, as a player, you're going to be like, 'Why are we doing this?' Especially the younger guys. But you've just got to buy in. He stressed that early on. Buy in, and we'll change this university."

As painful as the season was, looking back it was a necessary step back. It would have been great to go win a championship—SEC or more—but absent that, another 10-win season may have reinforced complacency, according to people around the program. But losing five games, including at home to the worst program in the conference and at home to the in-state archrival, provided a jolt. That may have been a negative jolt with players questioning the competence of the staff. But enough core players—outgoing seniors like Brandon Kublanow and budding leaders like the ones who formed the nucleus of the 2017 team—saw this the way Smart saw it. It was the classic method of Parcells, the mentor of Bill Belichick, who was the mentor of Saban, to break it down and then rebuild it. "We needed that year for sure," Bellamy said.

As rough as it all was, it may have proved to be for the best. "What if that junior year we had gone to the SEC Championship Game and lost? Would I have been satisfied enough to say: 'You know what, that was a good year. I'm gone,'" Bellamy said. "We didn't want to be known as the one of the worst Georgia teams ever. C'mon, Sony, Chubb, and Roquan all started, and all anybody remembers about that team is they went 8–5 and lost to Vanderbilt on Homecoming. We want our legacy to be way, way more than that."

8

The Crucial Month

DAVIN BELLAMY AND SONY MICHEL HAD A COMMU-
nications class together during fall semester of the 2016 season. They were sitting in the back of the room next to each other
one day late that semester when Bellamy leaned over to his teammate. "Yeah bro, I'm probably outta here," Bellamy told Michel. "I'm
beat up. I'm just outta here, man."

Michel nodded. He understood. He was leaning that way, too.
The prevailing assumption—inside the program, among the fan-
base, and among NFL teams scouting the college ranks—was that
Michel and Nick Chubb and probably others would be leaving
Georgia after that season. Running backs, who take more hits than
any other position and only have so many years to make money
taking those hits, don't tend to stay around longer in college than
they need to stay. Todd Gurley hadn't. Keith Marshall hadn't.
Knowshon Moreno left with two years left of eligibility. Even if
Michel and Chubb were only projected as mid-round picks, they
could still make an NFL team, maybe even start, and make some
money along the way.

Chubb, in fact, had decided in early December that he was going
to leave. He just hadn't announced it. As with many things, Chubb
was content not to share news with the outside world, including
his good buddy and fellow tailback, Michel.

Bellamy and Lorenzo Carter were also expected to seriously
consider it. A great athlete with a sculpted body and a smart
kid with a glowing smile, Carter was a pro scout's dream. He
had been a five-star recruit and long considered a three-and-out
player. Bellamy wasn't the star that the other three were, but he
was also wrapping up his fourth year and had a strong junior

109

season. It seemed the right time to turn pro and strike while the iron was hot.

But the more the four juniors thought about it, the more they studied the early feedback they were getting from the NFL, the more they talked with each other, the more they thought about not doing what everyone expected. Every player had his own personal reason. For Chubb it took making the decision to leave to realize he didn't actually want to. He got a gnawing feeling he was making the wrong decision. "It just didn't feel right. I felt like if I needed to leave, I'd feel it and be able to accept it and move on," Chubb said. "Something kept telling me, *Nick, maybe not right now. It's not the right time*...It all came back to the kind of person I am, to not just leave because things aren't going your way. But to fight through your problems and the adversity, and that's what I feel I did."

Michel hadn't gone as far as Chubb in deciding to leave, but he had come close, and he also got the same feeling. Like Chubb, he felt pushback. Coming back for a senior year when they had each already done so much would go against what so many Georgia tailbacks before them had done: Herschel Walker, Hearst, Gurley, Moreno, and so on had all left with eligibility left. Chubb and Michel would be sacrificing a year of earnings and risk their careers in the name of...what, exactly? This was a seven-win Georgia team with a rookie head coach, who some were saying looked in over his head. Why come back to that? With all his great measurables, Carter was hearing the same thing: get the money. Even if you don't get drafted that high and it's only some money, it's still money.

They weren't the only four considering it. Safety Dominick Sanders, defensive back Aaron Davis, and offensive lineman Isaiah Wynn were also mulling it. Receiver/kick returner Isaiah McKenzie had some pro stock and was also dealing with an academic matter that was jeopardizing his eligibility. It looked like a mass exodus could be afoot. "I didn't expect a lot of us to come back," Bellamy said, looking back a few years later. "A lot of us were out of there."

But it wasn't just a cold-blooded business decision for any of them, they recalled later. Even amidst this disappointing Year One of the Kirby Smart era, the harder practices, and the painful losses, the juniors were looking around and starting to realize they weren't crazy about leaving this place, at least not quite yet. "We just started thinking: *This could be a special team*," Bellamy said.

Bellamy would be the last one to "come around," as he put it. His stock may have been the lowest among the four, but he was also a fourth-year player, one year older than the rest, closer to his degree, and returning to college meant sacrificing another year of salary on the front end. But Carter kept lobbying him, whether it was while they were doing something football related or hanging out downtown. "I need you for this last year," Carter told his fellow outside linebacker.

Bellamy finally relented. And when he told his head coach, it wasn't in any momentous sit-down meeting. It was near the end of a practice, as they were switching to a new drill. Bellamy jogged by Smart and told him his decision. "Yeah, I'm staying," Bellamy told Smart.

The coach smiled back. That was it. "Then we ended up having a great-ass practice," Bellamy said.

Smart choreographed the announcement for effect. It was revealed after practice on December 13 during a regularly-scheduled bowl practice. Showing his savvy PR chops, Smart began by announcing that three other players—Shaquery Wilson, Juwuan Briscoe, and Rico McGraw—would be transferring. Normally, that was big news.

But Smart knew that on this day the news would be buried. Word had already started to leak out, so a reporter asked Smart about an update on players contemplating the NFL. "There may be word on that soon," Smart answered with a gleam in his eye.

A few minutes later, Smart decided it was time. He looked at the reporter who had asked the question. "You asked whether it would be soon. Well, it's now," Smart said. "We've got some guys that want to come in and make a statement."

And in walked Chubb, Michel, Carter, and Bellamy, and Smart announced off-handedly that all four had decided to come back. Michel spoke first followed by Carter, Bellamy, and Chubb. No one said anything too Earth-shattering, but they didn't need to. The decision itself was enough, especially packaged together, to make it look like one grand buy-in rather than what it really was: a group of individual decisions.

Perhaps nobody was more surprised than some of their own teammates. There had been no big moment behind the scenes where the four announced their return to their teammates, who basically found out the way everybody else did. "It was really a shock," Jeb Blazevich said. "Because the rest of us were like, 'You did what you did here. It is what it is. I don't know how we're going to do next year. You're amazing guys, you're amazing players, go get yours.' And then they come back, and it's like: 'Oh they really do care! Well, if they're willing to buy in for another year, then why not me?'"

It was the most demonstrative act of leadership, Blazevich added, because they put their money on the line. It reverberated around the team and set the tone for the following season, when Georgia became a veteran-laden team led mostly by seniors. Had Chubb and Michel left, had Carter and Bellamy left, there would have been talented players behind them, but the leadership on each side of the ball would have been different. And who knows whether the mix would have been productive.

It's forgotten now that if Chubb, Michel, and others had returned, they probably still would have been NFL starters—though perhaps not—but their legacy at Georgia would have been that of good players, who, like others, could not get their team to the promised land. They did return in part to improve their own stock, but they also returned for a larger purpose. "To be that unselfish, to come back, understand that we want to do something bigger," said Aaron Davis, who was facing his own decision on his future that December, "we don't want to leave our legacy the way it is now. We want to change that. That definitely showed us because even in years past we weren't accustomed to being satisfied with going to the Liberty Bowl."

It was one thing for players to get in front of the cameras and say that people were buying in. But it was hard for anyone on the outside—or really the inside—to believe that without evidence. It sounded like empty words or first-year coach speak. But when the four juniors stood in front of the media to announce they were returning, it was proof. It was a seminal moment in Smart's tenure and for the program in general. "That's when you really started to see the program change," Bellamy said.

* * *

Georgia had accepted a bid—well, been assigned to, thanks to its rather mediocre record—the Liberty Bowl, a third-tier bowl the team had last been to in 2010 during the worst season of the Mark Richt era. That week in Memphis in 2010, which capped my first full season on the Georgia beat, had been rather miserable. It was cold and rainy, a dreary atmosphere befitting a dreary game, where Georgia fell 10–6 to Central Florida and couldn't get out of Memphis soon enough.

But the trip six years later felt different from the beginning. The weather was better. So was the atmosphere around the team, whose spirits had been buoyed by what happened earlier in the month. There was more spark, more life around the team in the preparation for the bowl in Athens and then when they arrived in Memphis. "We want to start this process now," Aaron Davis said years later, describing the mentality going into the game. "We want to show that: yeah, TCU is a good team, but we're a good team, too. This is what's going to propel us and get us off to a great start that will lead to next season. And then we'll see where next season takes us."

Georgia's opponent, Texas Christian, was also coming off a drab season, having gone 6–6, losing four of its last six in the regular season. But the Horned Frogs had some talent. They had finished the 2015 season ranked No. 7 in the country, and head coach Gary Patterson was considered one of the sharpest minds in the country. His name had been thrown around by national media types as someone Georgia should have pursued instead of Kirby Smart since Patterson was a proven winner at a smaller program and surely could elevate a program with the resources of Georgia and wouldn't have to learn on the job the way a rookie head coach would. The way that year had gone at Georgia had not done much to counter that argument.

But this day would belong to the rookie head coach. Or more accurately it would belong to a star-crossed sophomore defensive tackle. Georgia scored first on a Sony Michel touchdown run early in the first quarter, but then TCU ran off 16 straight points behind its quarterback, Kenny Hill, a former Texas A&M quarterback who for one game in an earlier season had been a Heisman candidate and earned the nickname Kenny Thrill. His fortunes had gone downhill after that, and they would go downhill in this game, too.

Michel scored again late in the half, taking a pass from Jacob Eason and going 33 yards, making it a two-point game at the half. Eason found Javon Wims for a short touchdown pass in the third quarter to give Georgia back the lead, but Hill responded with another touchdown pass to put TCU back ahead. Then Rodrigo Blankenship nailed a 30-yard field goal to give Georgia a one-point lead early in the fourth quarter.

Georgia's defense then took over. Or more appropriately, Trenton Thompson took over. Considered one of the top prospects in the country out of Albany, Georgia, tucked in the southwest corner of the state, an hour east of Kirby Smart's hometown of Bainbridge, Thompson was a five-star prospect in Mark Richt's last class. It was another southwest Georgia native, Mike Bobo, who helped lead the way to land Thompson before Bobo left for Colorado State. Everybody eventually wanted Thompson, but this was a case of Georgia coaches—helped by Bobo's connections—being the first to offer Thompson, who committed in August of 2014 and never swayed. Thompson's freshman year was rather quiet. He started for the first time against Alabama, but he mostly shared time and finished with 25 tackles. He played more as a sophomore, though still had not become a star, and entered the Liberty Bowl with just two sacks.

He would add considerably to that total against TCU. Squirming and pushing his way through into the backfield, Thompson recorded three sacks, taking over in a way that everyone had envisioned when he was given the five-star label. He was named the game's MVP.

Georgia's offense, meanwhile, proceeded to spend the fourth quarter running the ball down TCU's throat. Nick Chubb's 13-yard touchdown run with 2:48 left made it 31–23, which was the final score. TCU's offense was unable to do anything against Thompson and Georgia's defense. Smart was ecstatic. That fourth quarter showed everything Smart wanted to be: bigger and stronger up front and to be able to ram it down the middle.

It was also manifestation of Scott Sinclair and Ed Ellis' strength and conditioning program. Georgia players were still feeling great down the stretch of the game, as the opponent was getting gassed. It was the same thing that had happened against North Carolina in the season opener. The very first game and the very last game, which both came with long periods of preparation, had confirmed Smart's plan. Now they had to figure out how to master all the games in between.

Something else happened during Georgia's bowl preparation: the indoor facility opened.

Well, not officially. Complete with a ribbon cutting, the ground-breaking ceremony wouldn't happen until early February. But in mid-December of 2016, the facility was ready enough to use. So Smart led the team in a practice there. It was almost symbolic: everything was about to get better.

Dominick Sanders, the junior safety who had also been contemplating the jump to the pros, decided before the game that he would return for his senior season. That was more good news even if the final play of Sanders' career would go down in program and college football lore for the wrong reason.

Isaiah McKenzie did turn pro, announcing so in the minutes after the bowl game. This was a surprise, as McKenzie wasn't considered a surefire prospect. (When McKenzie told me after the game, simply saying, "Yeah, I'm declaring," I had to get him to repeat it a couple times to be sure.) But McKenzie didn't have too much of a choice. His academic situation, the details of which are still murky, left his eligibility enough of a question that the safest move was actually to turn pro. McKenzie turned out to be Georgia's *only* draft pick in the 2016 draft, but he still only went in the fifth round. He had been Georgia's most dynamic offensive player and a special teams weapon, but he would also turn out to be replaceable.

Davis, meanwhile, was also among those who decided to come back, even though he had graduated. He announced his decision a few days after the bowl, becoming the last player on the fence to land on the side of being part of something they thought could be great. There was also Isaiah Wynn, who a year later would be a first-round pick but who hardly even considered going pro after his junior season. The collective decisions to return would do wonders for what Smart was trying to instill. "That was a huge message to all the guys that were incoming," Davis said, "to say that we're going to make the most of this season. So when you show up to these workouts, we're going to give it our all. And we're going to be in this together."

Through all of this, Smart's points of emphasis—consistency and structure—were finally beginning to take hold. The wins may not have piled up, some players may have resisted, but time has a way of overcoming that, as well as the inevitability that Smart wasn't going anywhere. Many bought in to what he was selling because they truly believed in it. But others bought in because they really had no choice unless they wanted to go play or work someplace else. The more days that went by, the more it settled in.

As a Georgia guy who didn't want to go anywhere else and also bought into the Nick Saban/Kirby Smart process, Kevin Butler saw it from inside. "If you have structure, then it's very easy for coaches to coach better," Butler said. "Because the players understand that if they do A and B, then you're going to get to C. When you have that, it builds confidence in players, and then they buy in. And then you can always create a structure that demands more. And Kirby and his system demand more from the kids every second that he has them. And he structured it in a way that they love it. They respond to it. And we see people are wanting to be a part of it."

The return of all these players would mean that more than 20 seniors would be on the 2017 team. That's an almost unheard-of number at the upper levels of college football, where the best players are off to the NFL before their senior years, and many others transfer out, seeking more playing time before their senior year rolls around. Instead, Smart was preparing to enter his Year Two with a core group that had seniors at tailback (Nick Chubb and Sony Michel), tight end (Jeb Blazevich), receiver (Javon Wims), offensive line (Wynn), defensive line (John Atkins), linebackers (Lorenzo Carter, Davin Bellamy, and Reggie Carter), and secondary (Davis, Sanders, and Malkom Parrish). So it wasn't just the amount of seniors returning, but the fact that many of them would be the best players at their position. It was a mix that would pay off on and off the field. The decision of those players had a monumental effect, speeding up the timetable for the program to make its ascent. "If that senior class didn't buy in, all of a sudden, Kirby's another year behind," Butler said.

Smart, a year later, spoke to those seniors and made clear he understood their importance: "You guys, you've got to know and you've got to be proud that you laid the foundation."

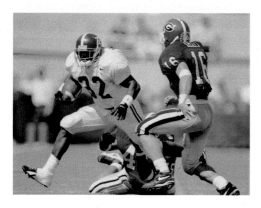

As a Georgia redshirt freshman safety in 1995, Kirby Smart gets ready to take down Alabama running back Curtis Alexander.

Kirby Smart had 13 career interceptions, including this one against rival Florida in 1995. (Getty Images)

Though he mirrors his mentor Nick Saban in many ways, Kirby Smart would create his own unique culture at Georgia.

During the December 2015 press conference announcing his hiring as head coach, Kirby Smart shakes the hand of Georgia athletic director Greg McGarity.

An estimated 93,000 spectators fill Sanford Stadium for Kirby Smart's first spring game.

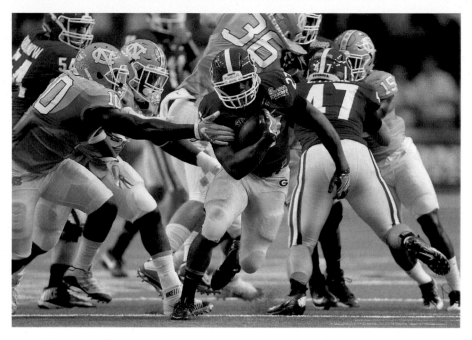

In Kirby Smart's first game as Georgia head coach, running back Nick Chubb runs for a first down during the Bulldogs' 33–24 victory in the Chick-fil-A Kickoff Classic.

The Georgia players celebrate their 31–23 victory against TCU in the Liberty wrapping up their first season under Kirby Smart.

Kicker Rodrigo Blankenship, whose scholarship situation became a bit of a controversy, poses after Georgia's Liberty Bowl victory in 2016.

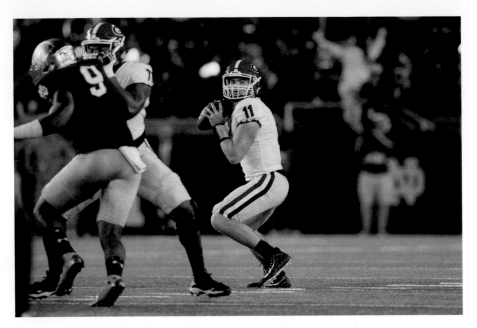

Starting in place of injured quarterback Jacob Eason, Jake Fromm throws during Georgia's 20–19 victory at Notre Dame in 2017.

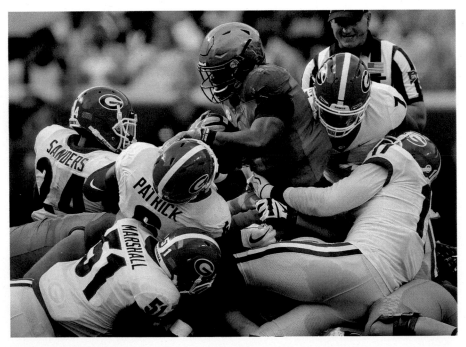

Georgia defenders swarm Tennessee running back John Kelly during the Bulldogs' 41–0 victory, which came near the start of their SEC revenge tour in 2017.

D'Andre Swift rushes for a 64-yard touchdown to seal Georgia's victory in the 2017 SEC Championship Game.

Linebacker Roquan Smith raises the trophy after Georgia defeated Auburn 28–7 in the SEC Championship Game.

Linebacker Lorenzo Carter (middle) celebrates with teammates after Georgia's SEC Championship Game victory, which came in a rematch against Auburn.

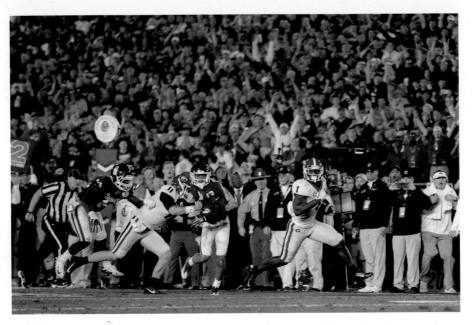

Running back Sony Michel scores the game-winning touchdown in the second overtime to defeat Oklahoma in the Rose Bowl.

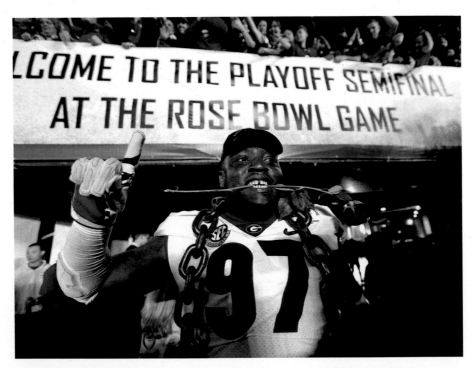

Defensive tackle John Atkins celebrates Georgia's 54–48 victory against Oklahoma in the Rose Bowl.

Alabama wide receiver DeVonta Smith scores the game-winning touchdown in Georgia's crushing loss to the Crimson Tide in the national championship game.

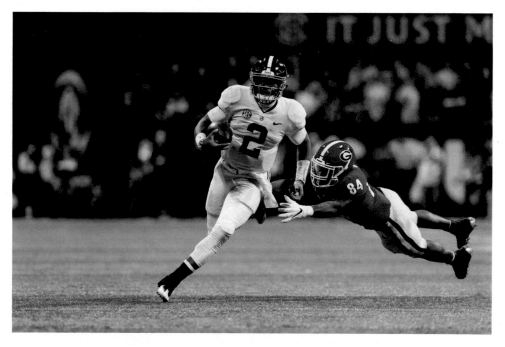

Once again facing Alabama in Atlanta, Walter Grant and the Bulldogs defense couldn't stop Jalen Hurts, who replaced injured starter Tua Tagovailoa at quarterback.

D.J. Wonnum (8) and Kobe Smith (95) sack quarterback Jake Fromm during South Carolina's double-overtime victory, a stunning upset during Georgia's 2019 season.

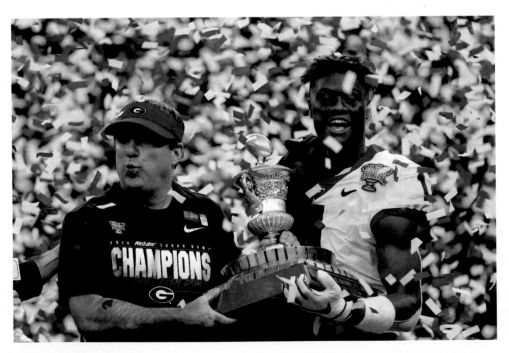

Kirby Smart and Sugar Bowl MVP George Pickens hold the hardware after defeating Baylor 26–14 to end the 2019 season on a high note.

9

The First Great Recruiting Class

to Georgia before the coaching change, but Smart's staff sealed the deal. All in all, it was a great job by Smart and his staff to hold onto and add quality to that kind of class, considering the transition. But it wasn't a true testament to what the new staff was going to do. That recruiting class of 2017 was going to be the key one, which would truly set the tone for Smart's tenure.

His recruiting philosophy, when it came to geography, was simple: trust the board. Georgia is good enough to have a national brand, and the various staff members had enough contacts in different areas of the country that they felt confident in simply targeting the best players they could. When it came to that first full recruiting cycle, that meant a mix of in and out-of-state players. It also meant a needed fresh start with some key recruits.

Andrew Thomas was a four-star offensive tackle from Atlanta's Pace Academy. He was destined to be a first-round NFL draft pick, was ready to start as a true freshman, and had a great head on his shoulders. The only problem is he was likely headed to Clemson. Thomas was receptive to Georgia, but the turnover in offensive line coaches—Will Friend had left after the 2014 season and been replaced by Rob Sale, who was not retained by Smart—allowed Clemson to swoop in and become a serious contender. But Sam Pittman worked his magic. Thomas' position coach at Pace Academy, Kevin Johnson, said: "If Coach Pittman was at, say, Clemson, I think Coach Pittman could have pulled Andrew in to go to Clemson. I'm not knocking anybody. I'm just saying that relationship they built [with] Andrew would have followed him anywhere."

That was an in-state player, but Pittman also worked his magic on a player that truly showed his and Georgia's reach. A huge athlete with plenty of raw ability that just needed to be honed, Isaiah Wilson was from Brooklyn, New York. Michigan, Notre Dame, and many others pursued Wilson in a national search, as it usually goes with top prospects from New York, which doesn't have its own dominant college football program. Pittman swooped in and worked his magic again. In a ceremony at his high school that was viewed by so many that the web stream crashed several times—Brandon Kublanow and several other Georgia players were among those cursing as they tried to watch—Wilson announced for the Bulldogs.

Then there was Swift and his mother's shepherd's pie. Smart and McGee's efforts were one thing, as was Georgia's vaunted history at running back. But what may have really made the difference was the 93K day. Swift was among the recruits there that day and later said that seeing a full stadium that day turned things for him. Swift, who had been involved with Ohio State, Clemson, and Alabama, chose the program that wowed him with the spring game atmosphere. Swift also brought with him a nice extra. Mark Webb, another Philadelphia native and Swift's cousin, signed with Georgia as a receiver but would eventually switch to defensive back and became a pretty good one.

Glenn Schumann, the wunderkind coach who had been Smart's behind-the-scenes analyst, also started showing his recruiting chops, as he and Smart reached into their Alabama connections to lure a future starter: Monty Rice, an inside linebacker from Madison, Alabama. Rice committed to LSU at first, but within minutes of publicly doing so, he had retreated to a private room and called Georgia coaches to say he didn't feel good about it. Instead of de-committing and publicly switching to Georgia, Rice instead just showed up at Georgia when the spring semester began, enrolled, and became a Bulldog.

Then there was Jake Fromm. The process of evaluating and then offering quarterbacks is arduous and results in more than a few disagreements. Those differences in evaluations can turn the fortunes of programs and coaching staffs, such as when Georgia under Mark Richt and Mike Bobo were too late to decide that Deshaun Watson (from down the road in Gainesville, Georgia) would've been a perfect fit for their offense. Although Bobo made a noble effort, Clemson had already won Watson's heart.

Fromm was also in Georgia's backyard. Warner Robins is a couple hours south of campus. He grew up a huge Georgia fan and wanted to go there. But when evaluating the quarterback class for 2017, Richt and offensive coordinator Brian Schottenheimer had gone a different direction. They felt they had Jacob Eason in their grasp anyway but also preferred a couple other prospects: Bailey Hockman and Jake Bentley. The latter was headed to South Carolina once Will Muschamp hired Bentley's father, Bobby, as an assistant coach. Hockman ended up committing to Georgia. Fromm, meanwhile, committed to Alabama, where he was attracted to the offensive staff and scheme, as well as Smart, the Crimson Tide's recruiter in Georgia. So when Smart got the Georgia job, it was only a matter of time.

Smart and Jim Chaney offered a reset of evaluations for the high school quarterbacks. They were not as enamored with Hockman, who got the message and headed instead to Florida State. That left an opening for Fromm, who was happy to go to his home-state school. Now with its own void at quarterback, Alabama turned to a prospect from Hawaii named Tua Tagovailoa.

When Georgia's class was completed, it ranked third nationally, which tied for the best ranking Mark Richt's classes had ever achieved. It was quite an accomplishment for a Georgia team coming off an 8–5 season. "This group is a good group," Smart told an assemblage of media that day, trying very hard to downplay the individual stars and the No. 3 national ranking while emphasizing how most of the signees had only visited Georgia and won a state championship at their school. "That's important to you guys," he said of the No. 3 ranking. "That's not as important to me—the ranking—as it is what kind of kids these young men are."

Georgia fans and national media members were more effusive. As USA TODAY college football writer Paul Myerberg put it while calling Georgia one of the winners of Signing Day: "Championship runs are built on recruiting classes like the one Kirby Smart and

Georgia signed in 2017. Just ask Smart's former boss, Nick Saban, who began a dynasty with the Tide's 2008 class.

So how did this happen? It was a good year for prospects in Georgia, and most of the recruits (including Thomas and Fromm) were in-state athletes. But out-of-staters Wilson, Swift, and Rice became three of the best members of the class, and a few others (Webb, receiver Matt Landers) also contributed, portending future classes that would show Georgia's reach.

There wasn't one magical recruit that made the class go, and there wasn't one assistant who was leading the charge above everybody else. It all just came together, thanks to a combination of organization and charisma. The charisma was largely Smart, and he set the tone around the building when it came to recruiting. Jonathan Ledbetter, who came in during the Richt era but had also been recruited by Smart, saw how Georgia recruited under Smart and marveled at it. "You feel at home there. It's not fake. It's real. He cares about people," Ledbetter said. "You know my story. He cared about me more than half of the people in my life, took chances on me. And that speaks volumes. He's like that with everyone. He's just that type of person and he recruits that type of people. And if he doesn't like you and doesn't think you're a fit, he won't recruit you. He only goes after the people that he wants and will fit in with the program. He's a tough coach and he'll tell you that. It's not blowing smoke and mirrors up you. He would tell you how it is and he'll be real with you. That's what you want in a football coach. You don't want someone who's a pretender."

But there was also the organization part of it. And Ledbetter saw and marveled at that part of it too. "They're just good at what they do," Ledbetter said. "They're on top of everything."

* * *

Shane Beamer had always marveled from afar at everything Georgia had to offer. Having recruited the state for years, he knew the oodles of high school football talent. He had also come to Athens as an opponent while serving as a Georgia Tech and then Tennessee graduate assistant, an assistant at Mississippi State, and then an assistant at South Carolina. He had seen the environment at Sanford Stadium. He had also visited Athens plenty of times since he was a teenager, whether it was to play golf, have a meal, or just visit with Mike Bobo. So he knew the community, the academic reputation of the school, and the other attractions.

Mark Richt and Loren Smith were once driving through campus during a summer day on their way to a function. As coeds walked around the bucolic campus outside their window, Richt turned to Smith. "You know, you'd almost have to work to screw this up," Richt said with a smile.

Richt didn't screw it up. Overall they recruited well, but they still hadn't recruited quite well enough. Part of Smart's charge was to improve that. "There were tons of positives going into it that you knew made this a great place to recruit," Beamer said. "Coach Richt obviously did that with the many great recruiting classes he had. So you knew you were going into a product that from Day One, that you have a lot to sell, but then you get in there and put the bulldog mentality in there."

By the bulldog mentality, Beamer didn't mean the mascot. He meant Kirby Smart.

Watching Smart in the locker room around the players, sideline reporter Chuck Dowdle saw the charismatic side of the coach that lured recruits. "When Kirby talks to these kids, Kirby gets animated, and you see it, and his hair starts flopping around, and those kids they just lock in. They just lock in on that," Dowdle said. "You sit there and say to yourself, *Damn, no wonder he's a good recruiter. He connects to those kids.*"

But it takes more than connecting. Rusty Mansell, the longtime recruiting guru in Georgia, said an assistant coach once told him that he had "never been around someone who works as hard as Kirby Smart. I don't know when the guy sleeps."

Smart would send texts all day long and at all hours of the night. "That's the way he attacks recruiting," Mansell said. "Those guys like him, who are what I consider alpha recruiters, that can never turn that switch off, right or wrong, it's hard for them to unplug because that's the way they are wired. I think Kirby is one of those who is just nonstop recruiting, nonstop relentless."

That was what made Smart so successful a recruiter as an assistant coach. Now he had become a head coach but was keeping the same mentality he had as an assistant while expecting his assistants to be the same way. This was a change from what Georgia had been used to under the previous staff. Smart put together his first staff with an emphasis on recruiting and he was going to hold everyone to a standard. Perhaps the only assistant not known as a great recruiter was Jim Chaney, but he was the offensive coordinator and brought plenty more to the table. The gregarious personality that he was, Chaney didn't really hurt the team on the recruiting trail either. Plus he was key to being able to bring in Sam Pittman, who became the best recruiter on Georgia's staff.

The bottom line: Smart expected his assistants to get results on the recruiting trails. He judged them by it, using raises as rewards and the threat of discontinued employment as punishment. "A lot of staffs have that guy or couple of guys, who maybe they're not great recruiters, but they're really good position coaches. I don't really see a lot of that at Georgia," Mansell said. "I don't think that's a long-term fit. There might be one of two guys that stay a couple years. But you've got to be able to recruit and you've got to be able to recruit your room and be able to coach them up to be able to work for Kirby Smart."

sometimes they get a tip, sometimes they're well aware of prospects being recruited by smaller schools and decide to be the first big school to swoop in with an offer. But the evaluation process—in person and on video—isn't just about figuring out which recruits to pursue. It's about following those recruits and deciding whether to cut bait or to pursue harder. After all, these are teenagers who develop at different rates. So the evaluation process is also about trying to find the good recruits as early as possible—hence offers to ninth graders and sometimes earlier—but also making sure that by their senior year, when they can actually sign, that Georgia wanted to still sign them. How is the player improving or is he not improving? Does he have upside?

That requires constant evaluation. Beamer said he watched more video of recruits in his two years at Georgia than he probably had in his entire career up to that point. It was like that for the entire staff. Smart himself was always watching it, whether it was on a high-tech big screen in the team offices or on his phone during what would have been downtime for other coaches.

There was not much downtime. During game weeks Friday morning for many programs was laid-back, as every practice had been held, and the coaches killed time until the team got together to travel to the game or the team hotel. But under Smart that meant Fridays were another opportunity to recruit. Coaches were expected in the office at 7:30 AM, and all they did for the next few hours was watch video of high school prospects. "Very, very few teams in the country do that," Beamer said. "But we were going to evaluate and know of a lot of people and have a giant pool of guys to recruit from. That was new to me. But it's great. You're making thorough decisions."

Smart used to remind his staff: yes, there are a ton of recruits in Georgia's backyard, and many more nationally attracted to the brand, but you better make sure that you're taking and offering the right ones because the ones you don't take are likely going nearby to Tennessee, Auburn, South Carolina, or some other SEC program you're going to be playing against. Perhaps for that reason, much of Smart's own focus when he watched film was the in-state Georgia talent.

Smart also constantly judged the evaluation skills of his assistant coaches. He called it a "quality control" look at each staff member based on their recruiting and how those recruits panned out or didn't pan out. "Look at every player and rank every player, and whether we get them or not, four years from now, we come back and look at those," Smart said. "We say: okay, who did we miss on? Why did we miss on them? Who was right? Maybe that guy is a better evaluator."

This evaluation process was part of what put Georgia ahead of the game. Smart's personal skills with recruits and their families and those of his assistants were certainly good, especially for that 2017 recruiting class, which came off an 8–5 record and had a staff that had been in place just over a year. But the work they put in during the rest of the process was just as important. They found players early in the process and adjusted their board as time went on, managing the recruiting class so that they emerged with the best 25 or so signees. This sometimes meant backing off a commitment if they ended up liking someone better at the position. Essentially, when a player was offered a scholarship or even committed to Georgia, the process was far from over. The staff might still have questions about him, whether it was his agility, lateral movement, development, or drive for greatness. "It was very, very thorough from the time you start recruiting a guy right up until Signing Day," Beamer said.

This part of the process was what made Alabama so successful, too. Yes, the Crimson Tide reeled in five-star players, and yes, the Crimson Tide pulled in one of—if not—the nation's top class every year. And yes, those rankings were per the recruiting experts and websites. But much of the process was symbiotic. When certain teams pursue a player or back off a player, it makes the recruiting services and writers re-evaluate their own analysis. "The hidden genius of Nick is the way he evaluates players and projects them really well," said CBS game analyst Gary Danielson. "No matter where he was, whether he was at Michigan State, LSU, or Alabama, his ability to project young players and know how good they'd be is a skill that might be unteachable." Smart was showing signs he had this skill as well.

10

Building a Powerhouse

I N THE SPRING AFTER HE WAS HIRED, KIRBY SMART WAS the featured speaker at a fund-raiser for the Magill Society, an upper-echelon group of donors to Georgia athletics. You need to donate at least $25,000 to get into the society. This fund-raiser was at the Capital City Club, a swank country club in Atlanta established in 1883. Its dress code states that "gentleman may not wear hats of any kind, shorts, jeans, open-toed shoes, or shirts without collars."

This was a private event without media. And Georgia's new head coach was going to be brutally honest with the donors he was wooing. Bo Means, a high-level Georgia donor and residential home builder in Atlanta, spoke before Smart. The gist of Means' message was that he was tired of Georgia spinning its wheels on and off the field. It was time to get going. Translation: it was time to do what it took financially. Then he handed off to Smart, who laid out what that money needed to be spent on.

According to a donor who was there, Smart told the crowd that he was embarrassed that his team was dressing in the same locker room in Sanford Stadium that he dressed in as a player in 1994. "And you should be embarrassed, too," Smart said. Smart also made another point. "I can make you two promises," he said. "No. 1, no one is going to outwork me and my staff. But No. 2, I'm not going to be able to out-facility anybody."

That was a direct shot at Georgia's facilities and its ability to recruit and develop players. But it was also true, according to coaches who had been through the program the past decade. Georgia was infamously the last SEC program to get an indoor facility, but it wasn't just that. The team had old locker rooms. The weight room wasn't big enough. There weren't enough rooms in the complex. Maybe it seemed ridiculous that programs like Clemson were building facilities with frills like water slides and fountains. But Clemson was also recruiting well and going to national championship games. Georgia was not.

Or it least it had not. The tide had already seemed to turn in Georgia's athletic department near the end of the Mark Richt era. Some of it was Jeremy Pruitt making his push. Some of it was on the upper floors of the Butts-Mehre building where Georgia's athletic department had a bright and forward-thinking chief financial officer, Andy Platt, who pushed for better and smarter spending before he moved on to the private sector. But by then Smart was on the scene, and things really started to change. The athletic department became invested in its head coach in a way it wasn't for Richt.

The recruiting trail required leasing jets and helicopters outside of town, including Florida. That never happened under Richt, particularly the helicopters. They had to use the school's prop jet. Georgia's travel situation for recruiting was a sore point. One spring Richt was headed for a speaking engagement in Atlanta. They flew the prop jet from Athens to the Dekalb-Peachtree Airport. As they were taxiing up, they spotted an LSU jet with the giant logo on the tail sitting on the tarmac. Richt and his delegation stepped off the plane and looked ruefully at the glossy LSU plane. "What's that doing there?" A staffer asked.

"Recruiting," Richt answered, almost glumly.

Things changed after Smart arrived. The recruiting budget went up for Georgia's football program and immediately began bearing fruit. If the team was going to recruit nationally and evaluate all these prospects, it needed the resources to do that.

But to be fair to Georgia's administration, it also helped that it had a coach who truly pushed for what he wanted. Richt wouldn't tell a room full of donors that facilities were poor, and they needed to donate. Actually, Richt wouldn't do as many private events period. Smart was different. He had those contacts with donors already, dating to his Sigma Alpha Epsilon days as a Georgia undergrad. He was a finance major from the Terry College of Business, a degree that required some smarts, but the new head coach also had street savvy.

Smart was often told that he was a businessman trapped in a football coach's body. He could scheme in the best sense of the word and work a room. He was an extrovert, a people person, a good speaker. And Smart's hands-on, micromanaging style on the football field also translated to raising money. Why delegate that to someone in the athletic department when he could do it himself? Mike Cavan and Loran Smith had already been the athletic department's biggest assets. They met with donors and raised money. Now they were joined on the trail by the head coach, who quickly zoomed past them in sheer energy and fund-raising prowess. Like Cavan and Smith, Smart could sell himself and his story: "I'm a Georgia guy. I'm one of you. Let's do this."

"There's a big difference between wanting it and demanding it," said one longtime Georgia insider. "He demands it." Smart learned not to publicly lobby the way Pruitt infamously did when it came to the lack of an indoor facility. "No, but I think he goes to Greg McGarity and says, 'I gotta have this,'" the insider said.

That could be big facility stuff. But it also could be seemingly smaller or involve low-level personnel. As a student video assistant, Frank Martin had wowed staff members with his production abilities. When Chris Conley made a *Star Wars*-themed short film in 2014 co-starring Richt and Todd Gurley, it was Martin who helped. Martin also helped put together videos for the football team and the university. He graduated and went to work in New York for a marketing firm. But Smart thought enough of him that he wanted him on the staff, producing videos for the football program. So he lobbied the athletic department to create a position for him. And Martin came back on board as director of creative media.

Recruiting, of course, remained the top priority, and that's where the big money went. That also included the infrastructure that Smart was putting in place, including the people who would help the on-field assistants. That meant personnel who could handle grunt work and other tasks, whether it meant stuffing envelopes, messaging with recruits or high school coaches, or administrative work that assistant coaches used to have to handle on their own. It included support staff who could do their own recruiting. While only the assistant coaches could go on the road recruiting, staffers could meet with recruits while they're on campus.

For example, Jay Valai was hired as a quality control coach. He spent the next two years at Georgia, and his connections in Texas paved the way for safety Lewis Cine (a top 50 recruit in the class of 2019) and receiver Tommy Bush (a four-star player in the class of 2018).

Nick Williams, a grad assistant, also pitched in with Cine because Williams was a former Georgia safety. Then Georgia had Bacarri Rambo, another former safety who was back with the team as a graduate assistant after Valai had left. It was the it-takes-a-village approach to recruiting.

Cine did not enroll until Smart's fourth year at Georgia, but this was a result of the infrastructure that Smart was setting in place from the beginning. Prior to that structure, there had been a resistance at Georgia to the idea of all this extra support staff. Expressing his reluctance even as Alabama and Auburn kept up their off-field hirings, Greg McGarity asked me rhetorically: "What do these people *do*?... Every job has to be justified."

But things started to change near the end of the Richt tenure. Pruitt pushed that along, but Richt was also buying into needing the help. When I asked him about support staff and the need for it at a press conference, Richt answered succinctly: "We will do what we need for Georgia to be successful."

By the time Smart took over, Georgia's administration was more willing to open the pocketbooks for these hirings. There wasn't a wholesale hiring spree, but more people did start appearing around the building, especially on that second floor. Smart was making more targeted hires aimed at the recruiting infrastructure. "Especially when [recruits] come on campus, those [staffers] are point guys," Rusty Mansell, the recruiting expert, said. "They're not just sitting around cutting up tape. Those guys are involved in recruiting."

This all got back to what Smart told those donors at the Capital City Club. Nobody was going to outwork him, and that included his staff. That related to one more strategic recruiting move, a subtle but important one by Smart with long-lasting impact. Along with what Mansell estimated was about 85 percent of the country, Richt held a "Junior Day" during the winter when about 150 to 200 prized recruits were invited, and they'd all spend the weekend in Athens and be shown around. Then Georgia's staff spent the next six weeks getting ready for spring practice. After spring practice had concluded, the summer was followed with similar big recruiting weekends. "Dawg Night" in the late spring/early summer was the biggest and often yielded big recruiting commitments. But the last Dawg Night had also been a bit of a disaster. There were many people in one area and not enough quality face time between Georgia's staff and recruits. Through his contacts in the state, Smart heard about all this and decided a more intimate set-up would be preferable.

So when Smart arrived, he switched this up. In essence he altered the recruiting calendar for the program and ditched the few big events in the name of making nearly *every* weekend a recruiting weekend but with fewer recruits each time. "Kirby Smart doesn't have Junior Days. Kirby Smart has *Saturdays*," Mansell said. "If you can come, then c'mon."

That made it harder for Smart's staff because it meant more time recruiting. If a recruit expressed the desire and wherewithal to visit on a certain weekend, someone had to be in Athens to host him and whoever came with him. Of course, it also meant more work for Smart because he usually had to be there, too. It didn't send the right message to a recruit if the big man didn't spend some time with him too on his visit, but Smart was willing to do it.

Smart also created what amounted to an open-door policy for recruits and their families when it came to the summer during NCAA legal periods. Instead of a few on-campus camps, recruits were told they could come by any time during the allowable 16-day period, according to NCAA rules. Georgia kept doing seven-on-seven camps but also emphasized the individual drop-ins. Smart now had to oversee all these visits, which he said was the biggest recruiting adjustment in going from an assistant to head coach. That quality control went back to Smart being a businessman trapped in a football coach's body. "I always relate it to Chick-fil-A. If there's a long line there, what do they do? They come out and take your order. We don't want long lines. We want to avoid that. We want good customer service," Smart said, speaking on Signing Day in 2017. "We're always trying to find a way to do it better than the other guy. We listen is the No. 1 thing we do. We talk to parents. We find out what they liked about other visits. We also do a lot of things in house from who's watching tape, who all is going to be able to evaluate kids and make the right decisions."

Jonathan Ledbetter, one of the players who watched this system be installed and employed, summed up why it was working. "You take his personality, his work ethic, you take the University of Georgia and what you have to sell with that," Ledbetter said, "and then I think the organization and the staff."

This leads to the eternal question: did all this increased spending happen because the administration said yes to Smart in ways it did not for Richt, or did all this happen because Richt did not ask for things that Smart did? There's a more nuanced answer: the administration was already beginning to turn the financial spigots on before Richt left. The indoor facility had been greenlit, and the eventual renovation of Sanford Stadium, which would bring new locker rooms and a recruiting area at a cost of $63 million, was something Richt had discussed. Down to the location at Sanford Stadium where he wanted it built and where it eventually was built, Richt and I personally talked in detail about it the summer before he was fired. But Richt was also reluctant to truly push his bosses. He sincerely believed in the idea that he was the employee and shouldn't get on a table and demand things. Still, even Richt got a bit exasperated at times. At one point as the process toward approving the indoor facility was slogging along, Richt told my colleague Gentry Estes: "It's about time to get that done."

Pruitt infamously weighed in on the indoor facility situation after a practice at the small, practically useless indoor facility before the Georgia Tech game in 2014. Pruitt spoke out of turn, ticking off UGA's administration in the process, and many within the administration still insist the indoor facility was going to happen the way it did regardless of what Pruitt said publicly. But whoever's right, the thing did get greenlit just over a month after Pruitt's statement.

It is inarguable that Richt had to deal with an administration that was not throwing money around throughout his tenure. When Damon Evans was athletic director, Richt at one point paid staff members out of his own pocket because his request to give them raises and/or bonuses was denied. Things improved a bit when Evans was replaced by McGarity but only a bit. They started to improve a bit more when Jere Morehead became school president in 2013. But there was still a pervading sense around the school—the so-called Georgia Way, as detractors derisively called it—that it was proud to be financially prudent and scoffed at the ongoing facilities arms race. That pervading sense was that schools like Alabama and Auburn were spending needlessly, while Georgia football and athletics in general could win championships within a financially prudent framework.

Smart's arrival blew up that mentality. It was one thing when Pruitt as an assistant coach was pushing for a change in mentality and had Richt's ear. It was another thing when the head coach, the one in whom that administration was now invested, was pushing for that change in mentality. "This is strictly my opinion," said Kevin Butler, though he shared an opinion that many did. "Mark Richt pushed more for his staff. Going to bat for his staff, that's how I saw it. Whenever he had a conversation [with his bosses], it was about keeping people, not firing them, trying to hire some more people. I know he wanted an indoor facility. Who wouldn't? I think when Kirby came in, you would hope that would be part of your deal: *here are the things that are going to have to happen when I become the new head coach.* And you get a buy-in from the administration. I don't know if that happened. I don't have a clue. But if I was doing it, those would have to be things that would be committed to by the university for me to take on that coaching position."

In fact, those assurances from the administration are not in black and white in Smart's contract, but multiple people say that was understood between the school and Smart's agent, Jimmy Sexton. And the parties had a willing participant in Cavan, who sat in on those discussions before Smart's hire. "Coach Cavan, his background is fund-raising," Butler said. "So put two and two together there."

Eventually, the change in mentality would pay off in ways that outsiders had said it could. The spending helped the football program, whose wins would make everyone feel more willing to part with their money, and everything built upon itself. Alabama's school president once told *60 Minutes* that the best investment he ever made was the millions he had put in Nick Saban. Some people derided that as a school president saying he had paid for football wins, but the president was making a larger point about what it had done for the school as a whole. "It's strategic spending," Butler said. "Alabama's proven it, and Georgia's really proven it over the last two years if you look at donations. Winning makes everybody happier. Winning makes life easier. The perception of winning goes a long way. It goes a long way to the educational side of the university. You donate to the university, [and] it doesn't all just go to new cleats. There's a lot of building going on over at the university...Football drives. In the South football drives. It's like Georgia's finally getting that second wind that we've been looking for since the '80s."

Georgia, however, would have to win first.

11

The Spring and Summer of 2017

R ODRIGO BLANKENSHIP CAME TO GEORGIA UNDER CIR-cumstances that remain murky. He was a walk-on but was what's commonly referred to as a preferred walk-on, who is encouraged to enroll with the understanding that he would be on the football roster. (The NCAA allows each team to carry an official roster of 125, though only 85 can be on scholarship and even less play in games.) Blankenship, who had been good enough to be picked for the U.S. Army All-American Bowl, turned down some scholarship offers from smaller schools because he and his family believed that he could show Georgia coaches that he should be their place-kicker and be deserving of a scholarship. And in fact the Georgia staff under Mark Richt thought that could happen. When Blankenship arrived he was the de facto heir apparent to be the place-kicker in 2016 after a redshirt year.

But a few problems arose. The first obviously was the coaching change. John Lilly had handled Georgia's special teams, but he left for the Los Angeles Rams and was essentially replaced by Shane Beamer as both the tight ends coach and special teams coordinator. But the other change was Blankenship himself, as he had a rough first season in Athens. His kicking in practices and scrimmages didn't wow the coaches. His quirky personality, which later endeared him to everybody, took awhile to do so. By late in the 2015 season, Lilly was throwing water on the idea that Blankenship was the heir apparent, saying publicly he was trying to figure out who would be the kicker in 2016. Georgia also brought in another walk-on, William Ham, who had kicked well at a private school in Macon, Georgia. And when the new staff came in and the 2016 season rolled around, it was Ham who was picked to be the place-kicker. Blankenship was relegated to kicking off.

Whether Beamer and Smart made the wrong decision, or whether it was just that Blankenship needed something to spark him to greatness, who knows, but the result is Georgia history. After Ham started to struggle, Blankenship stepped into the full-time place-kicking role and became a star. He went 14-for-18 the rest of the season on field goals and essentially won Georgia's game at Kentucky by making four field goals, including the last-second, game-winner. He became a viral sensation after that game by conducting the postgame interview with his helmet on, and his goggles made him a Georgia cult hero. He was named a freshman All-American. Blankenship seemed a bright story in an otherwise rocky first season for Kirby Smart.

But even that bright story would flip around. The Blankenship family was not where it wanted to be financially, and Ken Blankenship, the kicker's father, was very open about that. There were several reasons for it, including Ken (in his late 60s and retired) having to care for several children and having poured resources into Rodrigo's kicking career. So as he watched his son lift Georgia that season, he came to expect that scholarship to come along. It would alleviate a lot of the family's financial concerns. Rodrigo was also deserving of it, Ken believed ardently.

Near the end of the season, Ken, who once had been a copy editor at *The Atlanta Journal-Constitution*, was contacted by his former paper for what was supposed to be a feel-good story about his son's rise. But Ken decided to use the opportunity to go public with his frustration over the scholarship situation and issued an ultimatum: Rodrigo would have to receive a scholarship or would transfer. "Rodrigo has committed to the 'G,' but we are puzzled why Coach Smart has not yet committed to the 'R,'" Ken Blankenship told the newspaper in a follow-up e-mail. "His support seems to stop at the front gate of the scholarship house."

Smart was then asked about it at a press conference and tried to defuse the situation by ducking it. Those decisions are made after the season. But by then the comments by Ken were ricocheting around college football. A father was threatening to have his son transfer over a scholarship. Some were attacking the Blankenship family; some were attacking Smart.

Everyone was assuming this was headed toward a split. After a meeting between the family and Smart, who did not relent, it also looked that way behind the scenes. Smart was blunt, listing Rodrigo's strengths and weaknesses: great so far at kicking field goals and extra points but not great at kickoffs. Rodrigo and his father didn't necessarily disagree with it, but they still thought he had earned a scholarship—after all, there were 85 to give out—based on what he had done.

Ken kept up the public pressure. It came to a head when Ken sent an open, 1,536-word letter to three media outlets that among other things said Rodrigo not receiving a scholarship was "an injustice" and that it had placed a "hardship" on the family. That letter was sent out on January 5, 2016, and printed in its entirety by several outlets.

The firestorm continued. In the middle of it all was Rodrigo himself, whose own public comments had been measured and restrained. Behind the scenes an effort was underway by Georgia's staff to defuse the situation. The kicker spoke with coaches. They did not reach any agreement. It was only made clear that something needed to be done, and unless that something was Rodrigo packing up his things and leaving, then the kicker needed to do something. So he did. That night he posted a shorter statement on his Twitter account:

Dear Bulldog Nation,

It is of the opinion of many of you that my performance this season has justified that I be placed on scholarship. It is of the opinion of many of you that my performance this season failed to justify a scholarship. My opinion of whether or not I feel a scholarship is warranted is rather irrelevant, therefore I will not voice my opinion on the matter. Georgia deserves the best players it can possibly find at every position, and in order for this program to regain the national notoriety and respect that it so rightfully deserves, the program demands production from each and every position that is nothing short of impeccable. It is evident Georgia deserved better than what I was able to offer this season, and I would like to apologize for my clearly-defined deficiencies. I would also like to apologize for my father's interactions with the media this season. He acted without my knowledge each time, and each incident was uncalled for.

I have received unwavering encouragement, as well as my fair share of "constructive" criticism from all of you this season, and I hope that I will be fortunate enough to continue to receive support from the best fanbase in the nation, as we progress into the offseason and on into the next season. I hope that through this offseason I will develop into the kicker that Georgia expects of me. I love the University of Georgia with everything that I have to offer and I will continue to grind and work to become the athlete that the team deserves in order to be as successful as possible. I appreciate the love and affection that I have come across throughout the course of this past season and I hope that I can continue to earn everybody's trust and patronage as we move forward.

Sincerely,
The Kicker

And with that letter, the situation was seemingly defused. Blankenship was not transferring. He had distanced himself from his father's public statements. But he still believed he deserved a scholarship. And many in the Georgia fanbase assumed that Smart, being the hard-ass that he was, would give Blankenship the boot. That presumption was only cemented a month later on Signing Day. Wofford place-kicker David Marvin revealed then that he was transferring to Georgia that year on scholarship. Bye, bye, Blankenship family, many in the fanbase wrote on their Twitter accounts and message boards.

Smart, however, had not written Blankenship off. Publicly, the head coach continued to keep quiet. Privately, he liked the kid and wanted him to stay. He also wanted to maintain flexibility with the 85-man scholarship roster. He didn't have room then, though that could change later.

Kevin Butler had a front-row seat to all this. He stayed in contact with Smart the entire time the whole brouhaha was unfolding. Beamer was the special teams coordinator but tended to let Smart and Butler handle the place-kickers on and off the field. And when the public controversy with Blankenship began, it was Smart who took the lead. "Kirby was the head coach, Kirby was the one handling the scholarship situation, Kirby was the one making decisions on roster management," Beamer said.

Looking back a few years later, Butler viewed the way Rodrigo handled it as an important moment. "Rodrigo stepped up and did right by acknowledging the fans and his father, that that's his father, and I'm my own man. And I think at that point, Rodrigo grew up very quickly, matured very quickly, and kind of got out of the parental shadow," Butler said. "That gave him a lot more confidence to work with and to go out and kick on his own…He had the ability, but mentally he had to learn to stand up on his own two feet."

Acting as the student-assistant kicking coach, Butler thought he was able to work more with Blankenship on "thinking like a

for the Sanford Stadium west end project, which included the new recruiting area, the new locker room, and other small upgrades.

Smart, or course, didn't want it to stop there. But he was careful not to alienate his superiors by saying so publicly. During a press conference at the SEC meetings in Destin, Florida, in the summer of 2017, I tried to pin him down on what other facilities he needed.

"Our entire focus is on this west end zone project," Smart said with a twinkle in his eyes.

A few minutes later, Smart spoke to a couple of us beat writers. "I'll talk to you guys a little more," Smart said, chuckling, "as long as Seth doesn't ask me again about facilities."

I asked anyway. Smart repeated his "entire focus" quote with a grin.

Even with the media, with whom Smart did not enjoy the most cozy relationship, he interacted privately to make sure the relationship stayed on decent terms. The public side of Smart's dealings with the media—the scowling, the not suffering what he saw as foolish questions—was an incomplete picture. In one-on-one talks, Smart was engaging, relaxed, and cooperative. There was one instance—I can't get into details because the discussion was private—in which Smart and the core beat writers hammered out a disagreement. Smart was more than civil and clearly understood our position, which made it easier to understand his as well. We met for more than an hour and smiled and shook hands at the end. This entire meeting happened without anyone else present. Smart politely asked his communications staffers to leave the room so he could talk directly with us, which showed trust in the beat writers and Smart's self-confidence. He knew how to deal with the situation. He didn't need help.

* * *

Years later, some would say they could tell something big was about to come that spring of 2017, while others only said that a more natural thing was happening: the Year Two effect. Through the history of college football or really any sport, a team makes a big leap in the second year of a coaching staff, as the new system and the familiarity between players and coaches sets in. The coaches, in particular, had experienced this at several stops, including Kirby Smart in his second year at Alabama, which went from 7–6 to 12–2 in Nick Saban's second year, and now it was happening in Athens.

All that culture change, all those harder practices, all those harder weightlifting sessions were settling in with the players and becoming more normal and therefore achieving their desired result. But some players think it dated back even further. "The biggest difference was practice," Davin Bellamy said. "It carries through now to the league where people don't like practicing. But if you practice hard, the games come easy. And that 2017 team, we practiced hard as shit. It was more physical in practice than in games, and that was against each other."

The offense was clearly better. The offensive line was clearly improved in Year Two with Sam Pittman, and that was before freshman Andrew Thomas arrived in the summer, when he basically locked down a starting spot before practice even began. The defensive players who had to face that unit in the preseason could tell. "We were like, daaaammmmnnn," Bellamy said. "I'm glad I'm not on the other side of this because I don't want to go against this all game."

It harkened back to Bellamy's criticism of the 2015 offense of not keeping it simple. This year's offense, Bellamy could tell, played that smashmouth style that Smart and Chaney wanted.

There was also the freshman quarterback. Jake Fromm had come in with some accolades, but everyone's expectation was that Jacob Eason was the story. Fromm was the insurance policy.

But he was quite the energetic insurance policy. "This kid's going to burn himself out," Jeb Blazevich remembered thinking as he watched Fromm that spring and summer, doing everything full speed and corralling teammates for extra side work. "I loved it. I was right there with him. But it was something where you wondered if this was going to stick because we've seen so many kids come in on fire and hit a wall and say, 'Screw this.'"

The veteran-laden defense was also forming defined roles with unquestioned leaders.

"There was never any jealousy, and everybody had their own role," Bellamy said. "Roquan on the field was the quarterback of the defense. *The ball goes here, you go here, da-da-da. Right?* That's how Aaron Davis was in the back end. He was an old guy. And I mean, he knew routes before other teams were running them just with how smart he was in the classroom and on the field. Then you had me. I gave the pregame speeches. When the game got hectic or a big moment or something, I could calm guys down. I could fire guys up. John Atkins was the anchor for the D-line. We had a young D-line, and he was the only senior there. So they looked up to him. So everybody had a role."

The coaches were also realizing they could step back more and let the players govern themselves, whether that was getting on guys in practice who didn't know the play or firing guys up in the locker room. And it was happening organically. In past years Georgia coaches had appointed the leaders. Now they had become obvious on their own. "We naturally grew into our roles," Bellamy said. "We knew Roquan watched film—more than me and Lorenzo, I can tell you that much. So we knew: I'm gonna listen to this guy; this guy watches more film than me. Roquan also knew that Bellamy is very charismatic, or he knows how to get people fired up. So he let me do that. And he knew John Atkins had a whole new D-line, so he let him do that. He knew AD had the whole back end, so he let him do that."

It was the best possible arrangement. It had happened organically. The coaches could pull back and focus on strategy, and the players could enforce the rules themselves. The year before players, who got up to speak, tended to be those who felt an obligation or were even told to get up. But as 2017 went on, it just clicked. "It's not: this guy is getting up because he feels like he has to. It's like, oh he has something good to say. We want to hear from him," Blazevich said. "How can I encourage and support him doing that?"

Bellamy compared it to the Golden State Warriors of that era because the close-knit squad was successful and lacked jealously among its myriad stars. "The most important thing I want people to realize about that '17 team is we were really a family," Bellamy said. "We partied together, we went to the movies together, we went out to eat together. That team was really a family."

Blazevich comes back to the consistent approach. He remembered back to the 2016 home loss to Vanderbilt. Players came in expecting to be killed in practice that week. Instead Smart kept it on an even keel and stayed the course. There was no reaction to a bad practice on a Wednesday by going full pads on a Thursday. The plan would be the same whether they were 4–4 or 8–0. "If this is the consistent process, then it makes it a whole lot easier for me to trust it and buy into it," Blazevich said.

The contrast with the same point the prior year—Year One of the Smart era—was stark. There were fewer, if any veterans, pushing back on a new staff. "It got to a point where it wasn't a coach-led team anymore," Jonathan Ledbetter said. "That's the teams that win championships, where your players lead the other players. And that leadership really came into effect and it really started manifesting itself."

The coaches could tell this was a different group, a good group. It had begun with the rising seniors, Nick Chubb and company, opting to return, and it had carried into the fall. This was a more veteran group, but it wasn't just that they were older. "Those older guys on that team, they were hungry," Shane Beamer said. "They were tired of losing to Florida, they were tired of losing to Tennessee, they were tired of seeing Alabama win these SEC championships. They were very, very hungry and very, very motivated. And once Nick and Sony came back, they were on a mission, and everybody couldn't help but follow suit."

The best teams Beamer had been around, whether it was Virginia Tech when it reached the national championship in 2000 or South Carolina reaching the SEC championship in 2010, all had great chemistry and leadership, but their best players were their hardest workers. Everyone could tell that was the case with this team.

But even Beamer didn't realize something truly special was brewing. There was certainly a sense of improvement, a better sense of comfort entering Year Two, but he had been in the business long enough to be only cautiously optimistic. Beamer looked around the offense and saw Chubb and Sony Michel being back and Jacob Eason in his second year as the starter and felt better. He looked at the defense and saw Lorenzo Carter and Bellamy back and Roquan Smith starting to make a lot of plays in practice and liked all that. He liked that everyone kind of knew what to expect rather than everyone being new to each other. But that was it. "I don't think I walked out of spring practice necessarily saying to myself, *"okay, we're going to go play in the national championship game,"* Beamer said. "I know we all felt like we were building, we were getting better, and we were putting together good recruiting classes. But I don't think we walked out of there saying we had a national championship team...But I think a lot of that honestly is just that's kind of the mentality that Kirby set that we all just followed."

There was recruiting to be done. There were camps to be run that summer. Nobody had time to daydream about winning an SEC championship, making the playoff, or anything that outlandish. There was too much else to do before getting delusions of grandeur.

12

The Notre Dame Game and the Rise of Jake Fromm

KEVIN BUTLER HAS A STORY FROM THE 2017 SEASON opener that he thinks perfectly illustrates Kirby Smart. Butler was on the sideline in his typical role as a very advanced student assistant, and his job was to be the eyes and the ears between special teams coordinator Shane Beamer, who was on the field, and the coaches in the box, including analyst Scott Fountain. At one point in the first half, the coaches called down and asked Butler to ask Smart something: could they put Mecole Hardman back for a punt?

The sophomore Hardman was a speedy and dynamic player but still raw when it came to returning punts. They had been working with him on, among other things, not running before he had the punt totally hauled in. The staff knew he had the most upside of any punt returner, but worried he would commit a costly error, so Terry Godwin was still the main punt returner. But this game against Appalachian State was seemingly a great opportunity to start giving Hardman some chances. Butler knew Godwin was the "safest choice," as he put it. But he had his marching orders from above (literally) so he approached Smart, who was skeptical.

"Mecole? Oh God, I don't know if he can catch it," Smart said. Smart thought about it a couple seconds. "Okay, if we get 21 points up," he said.

Georgia was up by seven at that point. Butler went over to Beamer and relayed what the head coach had said. But as they were talking, Georgia scored another touchdown. And in a matter of minutes, the lead grew to 21. And, sure enough, the defense forced a punt. So Butler gathered the punt return team and sent Hardman out onto the field. The punt went at him, and Hardman bobbled it ever so slightly. But he managed to fair catch it. "All of a sudden, I feel something from my right side and I mean fast," Butler said. "And I kind of look and almost flinch."

It was Kirby Smart, of course, and he was livid. "You [expletive]! You don't call this!" He said. "You don't put people on the field! This isn't your [expletive] team!"

Butler just stood there, not saying anything, looking at him. Butler had been around and had played for fiery coaches like Mike Ditka, but it had been awhile. So Butler didn't know what to do or say. Smart ran away, still steaming. Beamer walked by Butler and laughed.

"Oh, he does it to everybody," Beamer said.

That was of little solace to Butler, who was still a bit incredulous over the whole exchange. Halftime came, and when the team went back onto the field for warm-ups, Butler went out early with the kickers for a few minutes. Then the rest of the team came running out along with Smart, who approached Butler. This time he had a little smile on his face. "Hey," Smart said to Butler. "Did Ditka ever get in your face like that?"

Butler didn't miss a beat. "Yes sir," he answered. "But I was gettin' paid for that, okay?"

Smart laughed.

It once again showed Smart's ability to compartmentalize and move on. Players and other staff members—even media members—encountered the same kind of brushback. They had been on the receiving end of a Smart thrashing, but those did not linger. But for all the scoldings that Smart leveled—some of them captured on live television—there was a relative lack of turnover on his staff. Maybe the money helped, too. But people in other situations have said money wasn't worth putting up with a horrible boss. Smart, meanwhile, didn't seem to push many of his staffers away. "His emotion is true," Butler said. "Out there playing the game he's going to be excited for you in the good and the bad. They co-exist."

Smart was that way behind the scenes, too, according to Butler, whether it was in meetings or at practices. "He will get in your face, he will get up in a coach's face. I'm sure if he didn't like something in the mirror, he would get right up there in the mirror," Butler said. "He holds everybody accountable. That is just the best structured situation any football team could be in, that anybody knows they're accountable. The ones that don't think they're accountable are the ones that [screw] up teams. And it only takes one or two to do that."

During Smart's first season, it seemed like that hands-on intensity might be a detriment. Was he spending too much time yelling at somebody while missing something else that was about to go amiss? Would a more drawn-back, CEO approach (such as Mark Richt's) been better in some situations? Having been on that sideline Smart's first two seasons, Butler doesn't think so. That's where his structure, organization, and support staff come into it. "He has a communication team—eyes and ears—on every player," Butler said. "That's why I say his structure, and he makes the most production out of every second. I really mean that literally."

That goes back to being detailed with everybody he hires. Smart doesn't delegate much, if anything, when it comes to hiring support staffers. He personally interviews quality control candidates, video coordinator candidates, and so on. Every single player recruited to the program on scholarship is examined, and everything possible is discovered about them before they sign with Georgia. So why shouldn't it be that way with the staff members who roam the hallways every day?

That mentality spread throughout the organization. From Nick Saban, Smart brought the mantra that everyone in the organization had to do their job and be prepared to do their job. That went for quality control staffers and players every day of the week. Smart publicly and privately reamed out staffers and players alike because he was setting the tone that expectations were high for everyone.

"It doesn't matter where you are on the depth chart," Butler said. "If you're on the depth chart, you've got a chance to play. And if you don't believe that, then Georgia's not your program."

And when it came to next man up, that was never more critical than what happened at the start of that 2017 season.

* * *

Jacob Eason had loomed so large in the Georgia program the past few years even before he arrived. He seemed intertwined with Kirby Smart. Both arrived that winter of 2015–16. One was the savior of the program off the field, and the other the was savior on the field. And in an instant, it all changed.

It happened on Georgia's third series of the game with 6:30 still left in the first quarter. Eason rolled to the right and was decked out of bounds by Appalachian State defensive lineman Myquon Stout. Eason and his long legs fell to the ground. At first he got back up and limped slowly back to Georgia's offensive huddle. Then he collapsed. Trainers came out and took him to the locker room.

Jake Fromm was now on the field. The crowd at Sanford Stadium, which had been so amped on this warm and sunny evening, was now in a nervous murmur. Fans whispered to each other. Everyone saw what happened to Eason and everyone could tell it wasn't good. Up in the press box, Jim Chaney opted to keep the pressure off the freshman quarterback for at least one play, calling a run to Nick Chubb. It lost a yard. Chaney sighed and called a pass play. The game was still scoreless, and at some point, Georgia was going to need to score some points.

Fromm led them to do just that, completing his first two passes as a college quarterback both for eight yards. That drive ended up stalling too after Fromm's third-down pass missed its target. But the next three drives were all touchdowns. Fromm finished the game 10-for-15 for 143 yards, a touchdown pass, and no interceptions. Afterward, everyone was publicly behind the apparent new quarterback. "There has not been a moment that's been too big for Jake Fromm since he's been a little kid," Smart told the assembled media at his postgame press conference.

But privately the coach was apprehensive, putting his head down and sighing. "I cannot believe I've got to play another year with a freshman quarterback," Smart said, according to someone in the room.

Smart thought Fromm had potential. This was a kid Smart had watched since he was a pre-teen, had recruited to Alabama, and then recruited again to Georgia. When Smart spoke to the Athens Touchdown Club in the spring of 2017, he hit on a number of the traits about Fromm that would later bear out. "He's natural leader," Smart told the club members. "I heard about this kid ages ago when his Warner Robins team was playing in the Little League World Series. He was one of the leaders of that team. He's been a leader everywhere he's been. Watching him in high school lead his team is a thing of beauty."

But now this wasn't about pushing the starter. Fromm was now *the* starter. That's a whole other animal. Smart, Chaney, and the rest of the staff were not ecstatic. The plan they had geared their season around had been suddenly altered and right before a huge road game. Notre Dame was next.

The feeling among the players was similar. They had apprehension about a freshman quarterback and sympathy for Eason. "It was tough because it kind of felt like Eason went through his rough year as a freshman, and this will be his year, and everyone knows the kind of talent he is," Aaron Davis said. "And then for him to get hurt in our very first game, and we have to bring in a whole other freshman two years in a row, it's like...other guys are going to have to pick themselves up because we don't want to be where we were last year at all."

That was a rallying point, according to Davis, especially on defense. "The offense is going to have a little bump, and we can't be frustrated with that. We have to go out and continue to do our job," Davis said, "because we felt like, as long as we played well, no team could beat us."

The team remained confident. "We knew that we still had Chubb. We still had Sony. Chubb and Sony are basically 20 points by themselves. And we've still got this defense," Davin Bellamy said. "Offense sells tickets, but defense wins championships. And everyone was healthy on our side."

There was also Fromm. No one knows how a freshman will play when the lights are on. But he had an it factor. Even seasoned veterans on defense noticed it. During voluntary seven-on-seven drills over the summer, Fromm was running the show as a true freshman. He was calling plays, trying to get people excited with all the rah-rah stuff. "I was like, damn, this guy's a freshman, talking to *me* like this?" Bellamy said. "He was what, a five-star recruit? We knew he wasn't a scrub. But his work ethic was displayed and showed in Day One. He got a lot of respect from us the way he worked, the way he worked out."

By that he meant the weight room, where Fromm worked out like a defensive lineman. Nobody knew what the young buck would do when he was thrown out there at Notre Dame. But everyone liked his spunk. Everyone could only hope that translated to the field.

The offensive staff was also a bit torn. They hated losing Eason—even if it was just for a few weeks—and they were apprehensive about starting a freshman quarterback in any game, much less on the road, at what promised to be a raucous environment. But if they *had* to start a freshman quarterback, Fromm was not a bad choice. "You knew Jake was pretty special," Shane Beamer said. "I remember the very first spring practice in 2017 when Jake was playing quarterback. He's out there in his first practice, making checks at the line of scrimmage, changing pass protection calls, and things like that. And you're like...wow. This isn't your normal freshman. But that was spring practice."

The uncertainty at the starting quarterback position wasn't Smart's only concern. He was also focused on something else: Rodrigo Blankenship's scholarship situation. The controversy had gone quiet for nearly nine months, and both sides had essentially gone to their corners. Blankenship had done what he needed to do privately and publicly and had staved off the competition from David Marvin, the graduate transfer brought in—on scholarship—to compete for his job. Blankenship had won the job and made his only field-goal attempt against Appalachian State. He had also kicked off well.

Beamer was in his office early in the week of the Notre Dame game when Smart came in and shut the door. "I'm thinking of putting Rodrigo on scholarship," Smart said.

A scholarship became available after Chauncey Manac, a four-star defensive end recruit in the 2016 class, left the team early in the preseason. Georgia was now at 84 scholarships. There was nobody more deserving than Blankenship. Beamer had no problem with it. He knew it was ultimately Smart's decision anyway since roster management was the head coach's purview. But Beamer appreciated being consulted. They spoke for a little bit, and then Smart left.

* * *

The context of the game is forgotten now because of what Georgia and Notre Dame went on to do that season and in the ensuing years. But at the time, this game matched a Georgia team coming off an 8–5 season and a Notre Dame team coming off a 4–8 season. But it was still Notre Dame. There was the mystique. And when Georgia players walked into that historic stadium, the locker room, the field, they felt it, too. It would prove to be preparation for the rest of a high-profile season. "That was really our first taste of a large scale that year," Aaron Davis said. "A grand audience. We knew it was a night game. Everyone would be watching. So we were going to have to put on a show."

But first Georgia fans would put on a show. In a display that amazed objective observers and dismayed Notre Dame, the stadium was almost taken over by fans in Red and Black. This was a destination, once-in-a-lifetime trip for many Georgia fans, who had known about the game for several years and planned on it. Many plunked down their travel budget for the year so they could make a weekend of it, going to Wrigley Field on Friday night—where Georgia fans also took over, cheering loudly when Vince Dooley threw out the first pitch—and then going to South Bend a day later. I was on the field at Wrigley Field that Friday night, and the roar produced when Dooley was announced still gives me goose bumps. It was another testament to the reach and passion of this fanbase. It truly worked out for fans in Georgia. The Chicago Bears even hosted the Atlanta Falcons at Soldier Field the day after the Georgia-Notre Dame game.

In the lead-up to the weekend, there were plenty of anecdotal rumors that the stadium would have a lot of Georgia fans. Some guessed as high as 25 percent. But as the stadium filled up and kickoff was minutes away, it was obvious that 25 percent was putting it lightly. Nearly half the stadium were Georgia fans, and when the Bulldog players ran out of the tunnel, they couldn't help but notice and turn to each other in amazement. It didn't feel like a road game.

This game was remembered as the night Jake Fromm began his legendary status, leading Georgia to a win on the road in his first start. The reality is a little less mystical. Fromm had an imperfect night, throwing for only 141 yards, getting picked off once, losing a fumble, and his lone touchdown pass was saved by a brilliant catch from Terry Godwin. That one-handed catch as Godwin fell out of bounds came on third down and was initially ruled out of bounds before being overturned by replay. Had it not been, Georgia would have been down 13–6 at halftime instead of 13–10.

Georgia instead relied more on Nick Chubb and Sony Michel, who each carried it 13 times, combining for 136 yards, and D'Andre Swift also contributed a 40-yard run. This was the night that the formula emerged: a physical running offense combined with a play-making defense.

Notre Dame had a mobile quarterback in Brandon Wimbush, who usually excelled not only at running, but also using his legs to extend passing plays. Georgia's defense allowed him to do neither. Lorenzo Carter and Davin Bellamy kept contain on the outside, Roquan Smith ran to wherever the ball was, and Davis, playing nickel, also filled the gaps, frustrating Wimbush and Notre Dame's offense when it tried to execute its gameplan. That forced the Fighting Irish into a more traditional attack of handing the ball to the tailback or passing out of the pocket. Although there was some success, it wasn't enough. "It was really fun out there on defense," Davis said. "It was just fun to fly around out there. There were a lot of times we gang tackled. Bell smashed the quarterback a couple times. It was just fun out there."

Carter had a sack-strip fumble recovery late in the third quarter, halting a drive into Georgia territory. Bellamy saw it and thought: *I've got to get one for me.* His chance came in the biggest moment. Smart and his assistants often pushed the idea that football is a series of one-on-one battles. Bellamy's was against Mike McGlinchey, the mammoth Notre Dame left tackle who would become a first-round pick. Bellamy didn't rush on every play, but when he did, he was baiting McGlinchey, making the same move over and over—deeking left and then going right—before abandoning the move. At least for the moment. He would save that for the end of the game.

Georgia led by one. The final drive ensued. Notre Dame ran a few hurry-up plays and had a first down at its own 36. Bellamy was tired. He was worried Smart was going to pull him for a fresh rusher. But Notre Dame was running hurry-up plays, preventing any defensive subs. In fact, on what would be the final play, you can see Bellamy jog when the ball was snapped because he didn't expect it to be snapped so quickly. That, ironically, was fortuitous. "Somehow me jogging off the ball threw his steps off," Bellamy said of McGlinchey.

Bellamy reverted back to that move he had employed earlier in the game. He briefly went left. McGlinchey went there with him. But then Bellamy darted back right, knocking McGlinchey's hands down in the process. Bellamy was free and clear. Then he went at Wimbush. "All I remember is it got dead silent," Bellamy said years later. "I hit him as hard as I could, like I felt my head ringing when I hit him. It was dead silent. Everything was slow motion. I remember getting up, and they were fighting for the ball. And I thought: *Did I just do that?*"

He did. The ball had gone loose, and Carter initially jumped on it. The ball came free again, and then Carter jumped back on it. Georgia ball. The game was essentially over. "That was really a moment that turned our season," Davis said. "If anybody had any doubt, they were probably getting rid of it after the game. Because we had a freshman in his very first start, that was very monumental for us."

I was on the sideline for the ensuing victory celebration, which was surreal. Here were tens of thousands of Georgia fans celebrating at Notre Dame Stadium, the home of Rudy, Knute Rockne, the Blue and Gold. And instead it was Red and Black celebrating.

Georgia players celebrated with them, starting a trend that would continue the rest of the season. Players and fans—and coaches and staff—shared postgame joy with each other on other people's fields. Then the team made its way to the visiting locker room. Several players spoke first. Then it was Smart's turn. He decided to make an announcement. "There was something that happened this week, and I'm going to let him...Rodrigo, come here," Smart said. "I want you to stand up here and tell everyone here what happened."

Blankenship sheepishly came to Smart's side and very quietly uttered three words: "I'm on scholarship." The place erupted.

Excited after a big road win and newly confident that this season wouldn't be like the last year, the Georgia players returned home to Athens early on Sunday morning. Nobody knew Notre Dame would end up being as good a win as it was. And there was the still fresh memory of 2016, when Georgia got a seemingly big Opening Day win against North Carolina before stumbling later. The coaches, particularly the offensive staff, also resisted the idea that it had won a seminal victory.

Still, looking back years later, Butler said he had a feeling after leaving South Bend. This was coming from someone who had played on a Georgia team that won the national championship, on a Chicago Bears team that won a Super Bowl, and had been around Georgia football for decades. "The way they handled themselves up at Notre Dame, I walked out of there, I knew they were a special team," Butler said. "They had to have a lot of little victories in that game. And they made plays. They made plays. That's the mark for me of a championship team is when you have to make plays, they make plays. And it doesn't always have to be the same guy, but guys are making plays."

Those guys included Godwin with his catch, Bellamy with his sack, Blankenship with his kicking, freshman Fromm with his steady passing in his starting debut, the offensive line with its blocking, and Chubb and Michel with their running. "That's troublesome for other teams," Butler said. "That's tough to make a scouting report."

Shane Beamer was a little more cautious. He had played and coached on really good teams before. He left South Bend dissatisfied with how the offense played. "We just went up there with a true freshman quarterback and we didn't really play all that well," Beamer said. "That wasn't necessarily Jake. That was all of us."

Clearly, there was work to do. But Beamer did notice something as he took in the victory. "There was a little more confidence," he said. "We just beat Notre Dame on a Saturday night in Jake Fromm's first start when we didn't play great. We got a chance to be pretty good."

13

The Revenge Tour

NO ONE REMEMBERS EXACTLY WHEN THE WORDS WERE posted, but they stuck. There was a whiteboard in the Georgia football weight room, on which Scott Sinclair and his assistants often wrote a quote of the day or other such inspirational words. Sometime in late September or early October two words popped up: "REVENGE TOUR."

The media jumped on it too. The revenge tour began Week 5 at Tennessee, continued to Vanderbilt, and then after returning home to wallop Missouri (which Georgia had beaten the previous year), it was back on the road to Jacksonville, Florida, to rout archrival Florida. Three times in four weeks, Georgia exacted revenge for 2016 losses. And another awaited in the regular-season finale at Georgia Tech.

But before the revenge tour truly commenced came the game that made Shane Beamer think this season could really exceed everyone's expectations. Mississippi State came into Athens in Week Four with a lot of buzz. The other Bulldogs were unbeaten; had a buzzworthy quarterback in dual-threat (and Georgia native) Nick Fitzgerald; had a head coach in Dan Mullen, who had always won more with less talent; and had Todd Grantham. The former Georgia defensive coordinator was making his first trip back to Sanford Stadium since leaving for Louisville in 2014. There were all sorts of angles for this game, which was a night game televised on ESPN.

Georgia was higher ranked, having ascended to No. 12 after easily dispensing with Samford (coached by Chris Hatcher). Mississippi State was No. 19 after beating LSU soundly and in much more convincing fashion than Georgia had beaten Notre Dame.

The betting line slightly favored Georgia, but plenty of experts were picking the upset, including Aaron Murray, the popular former Georgia quarterback who was now working for CBS and hosting his own podcast. That did not make Murray very popular that week in Athens, but he genuinely thought Mississippi State had a chance and was not alone.

As it turned out, Mississippi State did not have a chance. Georgia scored on its first offensive play of the game. On that flea flicker, Terry Godwin beat his man downfield, and Jake Fromm hit Godwin perfectly in stride for a 59-yard touchdown. Fromm punctuated things in the second half with a 41-yard touchdown pass to Isaac Nauta. The final score was Georgia 31, Mississippi State 3.

Afterwards Beamer was about to go down the tunnel at Sanford Stadium to get on the team bus to go back to the Butts-Mehre. But he stopped when he looked to his right and saw Dan Mullen and his wife, Megan, whom they had befriended over the years at Lake Oconee, where each family had summer houses. (So did Kirby Smart and many SEC coaches.) Beamer walked over to say good-bye to Megan Mullen, who proceeded to gush over Beamer's team. "There's no doubt you're going to be playing in Atlanta," she told Beamer.

She wasn't just saying that to be nice either, as Beamer remembered it years later. The Mullen family had been around the league awhile and had come away convinced they had just played the eventual SEC East champions—if not more.

The stampede to the Georgia bandwagon by national pundits began in earnest after the Mississippi State game. Not only was Georgia looking good, but the rest of the SEC also was cratering around them, especially in the East. (Florida and Tennessee were in spirals that would see their coaches gone before the season even ended.) It wasn't even October yet, and the path was already clearing. Then came rout after rout, as Georgia crushed its SEC foes.

Georgia 41, Tennessee 0
Georgia 45, Vanderbilt 14
Georgia 53, Missouri 28
Georgia 42, Florida 7

Before anyone could truly appreciate what was going on here, the first round of rankings for the College Football Playoff came out. Georgia was No. 1 on the strength of its unbeaten record and that win against Notre Dame. The rankings came out on a Tuesday night, and I remember the first player I saw was Rodrigo Blankenship. "We're No. 1?" He said, not changing his expression, just nodding and looking ahead, "okay."

And Georgia won the next week and the week after that. "There was just something about it. The days were long, but the weeks were super short," Jeb Blazevich said. "Instead of feeling it out it was more: okay, this is what's happening, and I knew what to expect. It's more of a natural flow throughout the week, throughout your game prep."

The leadership dynamic was now playing out. It would become the theme for the team and the driving force for the great season that unfolded. It showed during games, when Roquan Smith, Sony Michel, and others got in people's faces, and their teammates listened and took heed. It showed during practices, when the coaches pulled back and let the veterans do the yelling. But it showed perhaps more starkly after the games and in the locker room. Oftentimes, the first few people to speak to the team would be Davin Bellamy, Nick Chubb, or Michel. Sometimes Smart would be the fourth guy to speak. (That would not be the case the following season. Smart would usually be the first and often only one to speak.)

Cameron Nizialek was at Georgia for just that 2017 season and noticed the tie between on the field and the locker room, where the best players were also the best leaders: "When the play needed to be made, those guys made the plays. Roquan makes the stop on third down, or Sony Michel scores the touchdown in overtime," he said. "That clutchness, that leadership, that everyone on those teams knew those guys would make the play, but even more than that, in practice the tone that they set. Roquan and Nick and Sony, those guys were workhorses in practice, and they kind of demanded the same level from everybody else."

Nizialek remembered that in one of his first practices with the team—a mere spring practice—Smith raised his voice at the entire team: "Match my energy!" "He's calling on the entire team to match his energy, match his intensity," Nizialek said. "That was really important."

Even if no one ever came out and said so, Fromm also had earned the right to keep the job. It was a gradual and yet still stunning turn of events. Everyone had planned on Jacob Eason having a big second year, and yet here was Fromm leading the way even with Eason healthy. Things were simply going too well to change back, and the locker room supported it. Credit for that fell in large part to one person: Eason. "That could have gone downhill fast on the team if Jacob wasn't such a good teammate," Blazevich said. "If he started to get selfish at all, one, I feel like it would have divided the locker room in a large way. And two, I feel like it would have negatively affected Fromm and everybody else."

Eason was popular in the locker room, especially among the offensive players, but he did not pout. He realized his time with the program was going to end, but he put on the bravest possible face, stowing away all his hard work and preparation for a year that would be spent watching someone else lead the dream season. "We loved him," Blazevich. "He was the dude all throughout 2017 leading up. He was the guy. He was the starting quarterback. It just switched so quick, and Fromm did a great job, right person at the right time to step into that role."

As the wins piled up, awareness began to build inside the program of what may be coming. It wasn't just the move up the AP and coaches' poll rankings or even the College Football Playoff rankings, which came out in mid-October. It was the love from the national media, which nobody could ignore. Players couldn't tune out ESPN, and even if they did, they would hear about it from friends and classmates. This was where Kirby Smart, Mel Tucker, and others were able to draw on their experience from Alabama.

Aaron Davis summed up the coaches' approach this way: "That was something the coaches really emphasized: 'We know the playoff rankings are going to be out there. If you can, try not to watch it. We know that you're going to have people come up to you during class. There are things you can't avoid. But block that out to the best of your ability and continue to put on your hard hat and come to work because just as high as you can climb that mountain you can fall right back down it. We don't want to be in that position where we're that team that starts out 8–0 and then ends the season 8–4.'"

This unexpected run of wins was marked by something else: joy. The perception of Alabama and thus what Smart was bringing to Georgia was this machine that was run in robotic precision. While instilling "The Process," Nick Saban was renowned for seeming grumpy even after winning the championship because somebody in the second quarter had run a wrong route or something. But that perception had built over time, as Alabama won all those championships. As this magical season began to play out for Georgia, there was this celebratory feeling because it was the first time. And Smart wasn't just letting his team do it; he was participating in it. They were having fun. They were reveling in the revenge tour often at other people's stadiums.

They won and celebrated at Tennessee, who had shocked the Bulldogs the previous year. They won and celebrated at Vanderbilt, who had upset them the previous year. And on it went. Helped in large part by Georgia's fanbase, which followed the team in such large masses to Notre Dame, Tennessee, and Vanderbilt, the celebrations on the road were almost as rousing as the ones at Sanford Stadium.

There was compartmentalization. They could celebrate on Saturday and then put it away and get back to work on Monday. "I remember telling the young guys: 'This may never happen to you all ever again,'" Davin Bellamy said. "'Getting off the bus, people everywhere, everybody's turning into superstars, people follow you on the road…You may never have this again, so appreciate it while it's here.'"

The public face of the team was the usual one-week-at-a-time cliché, but privately everyone realized what was going on. "That's when this talk happened. 'Guys, what we have is really special,'" Blazevich said. "'As long as we've been here, we've never been this good. We have something special here. Don't mess it up. Do your part. Keep selling out and buying in.'"

Smart also remained consistent. It was the same as the previous year, when he and the coaches mostly treated wins as if they had been near-misses, lucky results when things were still being done wrong. (In fact, Georgia was winning games by an average of three touchdowns.) But it was that same consistency that players saw in 2016. "He coached hard the whole year," Blazevich said. "After a win it wasn't: 'you didn't win by enough.' It wasn't looking at the scoreboard. It was: 'Did you do your job to the best of your ability?' And his point most of the time was: 'No, hey, I should've done this assignment. Hey, I should've done this pass pattern.'"

The coaches were also keeping themselves on track behind the scenes. Kevin Butler described what it was like in a planning meeting. It was a delicate balance between coaches being free to speak their mind and the head coach being the ultimate decision-maker and tone-setter. "They're all candid," Butler said of the coaches. "And Kirby is the leader of the room. There's no doubt about it. I think if they get off of Kirby's philosophy, he keeps them focused on what their philosophy is."

Smart's offensive philosophy began with a simple idea: he wanted to run the ball. In later years that thinking would come under fire, but in 2017 it was the winning philosophy. He would deviate from that when necessary whether it's because the opponent is weak against the pass, or Georgia's personnel dictated it should pass more that given week. But those had to be exceptions. And Smart's emphasis on sticking to that philosophy also went for what the script was that week. The offensive gameplan was drawn up on Sunday and Monday, and the ultimate quality control on whether they were sticking to that script was Smart. "If they believed that running the ball between the guards this week will win them the game, he's going to make sure they're going to stay with that," Butler said. "That's what they told the players and that's what they have to do."

The players can tell when their coaches are shifting focus, deviating from the gameplan. That can rub off on players and have bad results. So Smart made sure the coaches stayed with the plan. But within that plan, there has to be flexibility. After so many years as an assistant, Smart also understood that his own assistants had to be free to opine on the individuals in their group. The position coaches are the ones spending quality time with the players, getting to know them best, and getting a feel for how individual players will react to situations in a game. They would know if Brian Herrien, for instance, was ready this week for a few more carries or if Michel or Chubb needed to be preserved for the stretch run. "Kirby is the leader, but I think his empowerment to the other coaches certainly comes out in the meetings," Butler said. "If somebody doesn't think the kids can do it, if they think someone else can do it, they tell the truth."

Smart also wasn't necessarily my-way-or-the-highway on everything. He regularly consulted with his coaches. Beamer recalled late-night calls from Smart out of the blue to get his opinion on something. "And I'm sure he was doing that with other coaches too," Beamer added. "He's the head coach, but he was very good about soliciting input from people on decision-making."

In early November Georgia beat South Carolina to improve to 9–0 and clinch the division. The game wasn't really as close as the

24–10 score indicated, as the Bulldogs nearly doubled the Gamecocks in total yardage and time of possession. Still, it was the closest anybody had been to Georgia since the Notre Dame game. Nobody was very alarmed, though. And the highlight of the day came that night when Kentucky lost, officially clinching the SEC East for the Bulldogs. Georgia was going to Atlanta just as Megan Mullen had predicted after Week Four. But first Georgia had to go to Auburn.

* * *

There were signs that week. Kirby Smart seemed a little more terse in his press conferences, particularly on Tuesday. And behind the scenes, he told the team he didn't like the way it looked. "This was the worst practice you've ever had as a team," Smart told the players, according to Jonathan Ledbetter. "And if we don't get it together, we're going to go get our asses kicked."

They did. The Auburn game was a wheels-come-off situation. It was cold. It was a hostile environment. And Georgia committed turnovers and penalties—more than any game that season. Auburn won 40–17. It was the most lopsided loss by Georgia to Auburn since 1990. "We were making mistakes that we hadn't made all year as far as penalties, busted assignments, turnovers. You name it," Aaron Davis said. "That was the absolutely worst we could've been and we honestly could've lost to any team in the country that season, the way we showed up. It was really a humbling experience for us."

Smart told his players that, even though the culture had changed and they played tough, they did not play composed. They had forgotten the discipline part. They had forgotten the lessons Scott Sinclair and his staff had begun instilling when they arrived. "That was the old Georgia," Ledbetter said. "We always played hard, but we didn't mentally come into that game right."

Auburn also seemed to put the knife in before and after the game ended. Georgia players recalled seeing them dance on the sideline, handing the ball to star tailback Kerryon Johnson, who was still scoring late in the game. Georgia players were crushed on the field and in the locker room. Usually an engaging interview after games, Lorenzo Carter frowned his way through one-word answers. Addressing the team after the game, Smart kept his response businesslike. It wasn't doom and gloom, as Shane Beamer remembered. "That's not who we are," Smart said. "That's not Georgia football. That's not the way we play."

He also told the players that all their goals were still ahead of them. They were still going to the SEC Championship Game. Speaking of which, Smart passed on to his players what had happened after the game. "I just shook their coach's hand, and you know what he said to me?" Smart said, pausing for emphasis. "'See you in two weeks.'"

That brought a few silent smiles. But Gus Malzahn's comment was more about Auburn's inward confidence, as it still needed to beat Alabama to clinch its own spot in the SEC championship. It was something else, though, that Malzahn said after the game that stuck with the Bulldogs. Video emerged of Malzahn saying as an aside to somebody on the field: "We sure beat the dog crap out of them, didn't we?"

Well, he was right. And Malzahn didn't know he was being recorded. It didn't matter.

That video would be played on a loop in Georgia's weight room in the ensuing weeks. And the locker room. And the revenge tour had another stop.

The morning after returning from Auburn, the Georgia staff went through its usual routine. The coaches graded film from the game and wrote up a report for Smart on things that went well and things that didn't. For once this season, the latter list was much longer. The coaches also listed the things that needed to improve. There was certainly a lot to do before the staff meeting at lunch. Smart's tone at that meeting stood out to Beamer years later. "Look," Smart told his assistants, "I really feel like that team we just played yesterday we're going to see again in Atlanta in a few weeks. I think they're going to beat Alabama."

Georgia was playing Kentucky that week. But before prep began for Kentucky, Smart told his coaches to look again at the tape from the loss at Auburn and to really dive in and analyze it well. "Let's have a plan while everything's fresh in our mind," Smart said.

It wasn't unusual to dissect the previous day's game. But they were even more thorough and spent even more time on it than usual because Smart had a hunch. On that Sunday they began to put together a preliminary gameplan for the rematch with Auburn, dispensing with what hadn't worked and coming up with an alternate gameplan if they could do the game all over again. "It's certainly going to be fresher and more vivid less than 24 hours from when it happened as opposed to two or three weeks when you've played a couple games in between that game," Beamer said. "So being able to watch that video of what happened literally the day before and be able to say, 'okay this was a bad idea. Running the ball versus this defense was not good, or this call on special teams, there's a better way of doing that.'"

Auburn obviously was going to tweak some things too, especially after playing some games. But Georgia's staff was now ahead of their eventual SEC championship opponent.

Meanwhile, practice got a bit of a spark. For as businesslike and composed as the Georgia players led by the seniors had been this season, at some point complacency can set in. "We fell too much into the routine of: oh, we're going to beat this team by 30. We're going to win by this amount," Davis said.

Players differ on whether practice was the problem leading up to the Auburn game. Some say it was; others say it was more specific to gameday. Either way something had gone wrong, and it was all a reality check. But even then the team and coaches didn't treat it as a drastic come-to-Jesus moment. There were no huge meetings. The energy at practice didn't ramp up. In fact, Davin Bellamy recalled the practices getting a bit less physical by design. There was a sense that players were beat up even if they weren't missing games. Isaiah Wynn was playing through a torn labrum. Bellamy was playing through a thumb injury. It was just time to take a collective breath.

Georgia got off the mat the next week by beating Kentucky by 29 at home. The players went into the locker room, and Smart got to the center of the room, stood on a riser, and yelled out: "I want everybody to take a knee! I want everybody silent!"

Smart began speaking. He didn't utter a single word about winning the division, knocking off Kentucky, or anything like that. Instead, the first thing out of his mouth was: "You guys are gonna hate next week! But you don't blame me! You blame those mother [expletive] over on North Avenue. Because practice is going to miserable! I hate them! I *hate* them! And you hate them!"

But in the middle of this tirade about Georgia Tech and in the middle of trying to avoid a letdown and putting the fear of God into his players, Smart did a mental 180. "Where's Cam Nizialek?" Smart said, scanning the room.

The punter, a graduate transfer from Columbia University, had been roughed up by Kentucky in that game and had to be helped off the field, though he came back to play. Nizialek raised his hand tentatively, as if wondering what he had done to incur the wrath that was about to come. "Bet you never got hit like that in [expletive] Harvard or wherever the hell you went!" Smart said.

The room erupted in laughter.

The team was back on track football-wise and mentally. The next week it went to North Avenue and took Georgia Tech to the woodshed 38–7. Georgia was now 4–0 against teams it had lost to the previous season.

Now it was full attention on the SEC Championship Game. Scott Sinclair and his staff were at it again, making sure that Malzahn's "dog crap" quote was still playing in the weight room and locker room. "That made us go ballistic," Ledbetter said.

Ledbetter had otherwise discounted the whole revenge tour thing. He saw the season as more of a "we're gonna show you who we really are" tour. But when it came to the SEC Championship Game, even Ledbetter was all in on the revenge angle. "We didn't care about the title. We didn't care about none of that," he said. "We just wanted to beat the brakes off them because that's what we worked to do. That's what we were supposed to do in the first game we played them. We went back in the lab and just grinded."

The game being in Mercedes-Benz Stadium helped. It was the first time most of the players had been there. It was definitely a different feel than Jordan-Hare. After playing Notre Dame, they weren't going to be in awe of it, especially a stadium an hour away from Athens and in the hometown of many of the players. And while everyone was aware what a win would mean—a trip to the playoff—Georgia players weren't caught looking ahead because they were playing a team they had lost to a couple weeks earlier. It was another way that losing that Auburn game had proved a blessing.

It didn't start out swimmingly. Auburn took the opening kickoff and drove downfield for a touchdown. Georgia didn't score on its first possession. Then Auburn took its second drive and went into field goal territory. "The mood on our sideline was: here we go again," Bellamy said.

The difference, though, would come on a play by Bellamy. It may go down as the little-remembered play that was the most consequential of that season. All that would follow—the Rose Bowl, the national championship, all that could be said about this special season—would not have happened if Georgia didn't first beat Auburn in Atlanta. And if Auburn had scored again on that drive, it would have reinforced that it was just a bad match-up for Georgia and continued to deflate confidence on Georgia's sideline. "When I sacked them in the red zone, that changed the game," Bellamy said. "If they go up 14–0, I don't know what happens in that game."

For Bellamy it was the same feeling as that game-clinching sack and strip at Notre Dame. Everything went quiet, the ball hit the ground, and then everyone screamed. And then everyone celebrated. The momentum had swung. It would never swing back as Georgia's offense got rolling. "That was one of the best games Chaney called," Jeb Blazevich said. "He created flows of the game that he designed. But he used it perfectly. So that was the game where you could really see what he could do. A really creative mind, he really understands the opponent. He feels like: there's nothing to lose, we've already lost to them, nobody thought we would be here, let me go see what works. And it worked great."

Georgia only led 10–7 at halftime, but the gap felt bigger the way the game was going. At halftime players sat around and initially had the unsaid realization. *We're about to win. We're about to be SEC champions. We're about to go to the playoffs.* It was the holy crap moment. Then they collected themselves. "Don't focus on big flashy rings," Blazevich said, remembering the feeling. "We need to get back after them."

Auburn almost tied the game early in the third quarter, but a field goal attempt was blocked by defensive tackle DaQuan Hawkins-Muckle, which proved to be the biggest play of the junior's career. It took until the fourth quarter for Georgia to truly put it away when D'Andre Swift's 64-yard touchdown run made it 28–7. But even before that, the complete inability of Auburn's offense to move against Roquan Smith and the Georgia defense made it feel like a rout.

When the SEC Championship Game ended, the confetti came down, and Georgia was crowned the conference champion for the first time in 12 years. Smart had done the same thing that Mark

Richt had done in his second year at Georgia. The difference this time was that there was now a playoff, and the Bulldogs knew they would be in it. Clemson was unbeaten and a certainty, and Oklahoma and Georgia were also surely in it as one-loss conference champions. They most certainly would be matched in the Rose Bowl, one of the two playoff bowls, because Clemson would be the No. 1 seed and kept closer to home in the Sugar Bowl. The only question was whether the last playoff team would be Ohio State or Alabama.

That was a matter for later, as the Georgia players celebrated in the Mercedes-Benz Stadium locker room. They were observing the 24-hour rule, celebrating until Sunday night, when they would start worrying about what came next. As the busses started pulling out of the arena to go home to Athens, Beamer tried to take it all in. He had played and coached in national championship games and been a part of other big bowl games. But this felt different. "That was the first conference championship I had won in my coaching career," he said. "So to be able to win that at a place like Georgia, in Atlanta, in your backyard, to celebrate with my family on the field, it was just very surreal and a special moment for all the work you had put in...So much joy and excitement but also the knowledge that there's unfinished business."

14

The Rose Bowl

D ECEMBER WAS A WEIRD MONTH. THE PLAYERS, COACHES, AND staff members were getting ready for the biggest Georgia football game in decades and dealing with the hype, family members, and tickets, and yet everything seemed quiet. This was where location helped the program. More than an hour drive from the metropolis of Atlanta, the city of Athens is isolated enough in the northeast part of Georgia that the team's facility is not a heavily-traversed place. In the weeks between the SEC Championship Game and the Rose Bowl, the players could essentially go on as normal and walk from their apartments to their classes or wherever they went and not encounter many people. Classes were over too, and enough players were taking online classes that for many it was just a matter of going from their homes to the football facility and then back home. They did not constantly encounter people asking about Baker Mayfield and the Rose Bowl. If they stayed off social media, they might not know at all.

The coaches had an even stranger dynamic. Even as they started preparing for Oklahoma, they had to also worry about something else: the next season. It seems crazy, but Kirby Smart had been through this enough at Alabama to know that it was necessary. They had to recruit. And in fact Georgia coaches had been doing that the previous week. The week of the SEC Championship Game was a contact period, when coaches could meet with recruits, so the coaches were flying out to visit recruits after Wednesday and Thursday practices. Shane Beamer flew to Illinois and was sitting in recruit Luke Ford's house two nights before the SEC Championship Game. "You couldn't lose a week of recruiting, even though you played in the SEC Championship Game," Beamer said.

But that year the early signing period, which the NCAA had put in for mid-December, gave it an added element. That created what

Beamer called a "mad sprint" for about 10 days between the SEC Championship Game and the early signing period. This was on top of final exams and award events. "Not to mention you're trying to get ready for an opponent that you know nothing about," Beamer said.

For Beamer that meant scouring four years worth of Oklahoma special teams film to try to find something, as well as old Auburn special teams film back to 2009 because Oklahoma's special teams coordinator had been there. It was a grind, but it also served as a constant reminder of what a big deal this all was. When Georgia coaches visited high schools, teachers, who were longtime Dawg fans, told them what this meant to them. Others reached out and said they were going to Pasadena, California.

Finally, the early signing period came and went, and it could really be about practice. The team had about a week of prep in Athens before breaking for Christmas. That's where the continuity helped the players on this 2017 team. They had been so used to the month of December being one of transition—2014 was when Mike Bobo left, 2015 was the head coaching change, 2016 was still Year One—that this time around everything felt normal. "We had a flow. It was the first year we had the same offense. It was the first year we had the same stability," Jeb Blazevich said.

Smart and his staff understood that there had to be a balance. They had to acknowledge it was a big deal and they couldn't force the players to be hermits. It was a playoff game, but it was still a bowl in a destination city with bowl-related activities and other possible distractions. Smart found the best way to manage a situation like that was to indulge his players, let them have fun, and show them he was having fun. That way if he had turn on the hammer and get serious, there was no pushback. There was an understanding that they had their fun but still had to practice.

So the team had fun. The team treated players to a luxurious plane ride to the West Coast. The jumbo Delta jet was outfitted with coves and beds. When they arrived in Los Angeles, they went right to the hotel, but the next day they went to Disneyland for a Rose Bowl-mandated activity and the players roamed free. The goal wasn't to cut out distractions. It was to minimize them, but that was still easier said than done. Never mind the usual noise and all the love players were getting in the lead-up to the game. Many of the players had never even been to Los Angeles. Then they arrived at LAX the day after Christmas, as the sun was setting in L.A., got a police escort to the Intercontinental Hotel Downtown, their home for the week, and saw signs welcoming them to the College Football Playoff and the Rose Bowl. It was hard to ignore the lofty territory. "It's the Rose Bowl," Roquan Smith said, "The Granddaddy of them all."

But they had fun. They went to the Improv to watch some comedy. They walked the streets of downtown Los Angeles. At Disneyland, Smart and a few players with the stomach to do so went on one of those drop-down thrill rides, where they strap you in and just drop you about a dozen stories. Sony Michel couldn't do it. ("I just don't like the idea of a ride going up and down," Michel told me later.) Nick Chubb did it, but the replay showed him to be more nervous than seemingly any time of his life. Sitting next to Smart, Smith clutched his head coach by the arm, and both the coach and All-American linebacker smiled but were probably happy when the thing was over. "The coaches did a great job of giving us freedom to relax and understand that this isn't the same scenario. It's going to be hard to mimic preparing as at home," Aaron Davis said. "Guys have a little down time to relax and get their mind off the gameplan, so that when we return to our business, we can be completely dialed in."

But when it came time to practice and prepare, they did their best to make sure that part was normal. Smart and his staff, who had been through these big-time bowls, knew what to look for in people getting off track and understanding when it was time to get serious. It was different running the show instead of just being an assistant coach. But Georgia players also knew that Smart had been through all this before, which gave his orders credibility.

The week in Los Angeles was one of the most fun he'd ever had, Jeb Blazevich remembered. The practices were mainly fine-tuning the gameplan, which had been installed during the Athens practices. "We had all this intense training. Then we had this chance to finally appreciate what it was for. And it's like: *Wow, this is a huge deal*," Blazevich said.

That point was again rammed home the day before the game, when they went to the Rose Bowl itself. Blazevich looked down at the grass and thought it was artificial turf because it looked so immaculate. He tore a few blades out to make sure it was real grass. Davis recalled growing up as "the biggest Reggie Bush fan you could find," so knowing the Rose Bowl was the same stadium where Bush had his big game against Texas made it momentous. "Then once I left the field, I understood, yeah, this moment is big, this moment is great," Davis said. "But at the end of the day, we're still playing football, the same game I've been playing since I was 7 years old."

The team was supposed to hold a walk-through at the Rose Bowl that day. But they didn't feel that secure—there were stadium and bowl staffers around, and Georgia people weren't sure exactly who was who—so they used the time at the stadium to just take it in and then went to a nearby high school for the actual walk-through practice.

At this point there was nothing left but the biggest game of their lives. Georgia felt prepared. Blazevich said he slept well the previous night. There was nothing to worry about. They were confident in their gameplan and cautiously confident in winning the game.

Then the game began.

* * *

The most anticipated events in our lives don't usually go as planned. So it was with the Rose Bowl and the Georgia football team, which could be as detail-oriented and organized as it had ever been but still had to deal with an opponent that created a series of events beyond its control. As calm and quiet as the weeks and months leading up to the game had been, the four hours of the game itself would be the opposite. They would spend years trying to digest the whirling blur. And as organized as the gameplan had been, once the ball was kicked off, it quickly turned to chaos. Georgia's most important offensive play call would happen when the offensive coordinator was in an elevator totally unaware of what was happening. The game-turning play would be made by one of Georgia's least known players.

Baker Mayfield and the Sooners offense were as good as advertised. Georgia's defense was being gashed. Georgia's offense did its share of gashing but far less in the first half. As halftime approached Georgia trailed 31–14. Oklahoma was doing everything that Georgia had prepared for and had played against before, especially Missouri and its fast-paced offense, but Oklahoma was doing it at a much higher level, and Mayfield was completing some stunningly accurate passes. Rodney Anderson was even more dangerous and he ran all over Georgia's defense. That was what disgusted the Bulldogs most. The problem was the pace. "It happened so fast—he was running all over the place on us. That's something if it happens in a practice, we're stopping practice, we're re-doing periods," Aaron Davis said. "Obviously, you can't re-do that in a game, so you just have to take what's going on, get some coaching on the sideline, try to correct it, and continue to play football."

In practice that month, Georgia's emphasis on defense had been on getting back to the ball fast, which they hadn't had to do, even against Auburn and some of the other fast-paced offenses. They ran a lot in practice, tried to get back in good shape. So they felt they were ready for the pace. But it was the Sooners' physicality that surprised the Bulldogs, who weren't ready for it. "We took them lightly," Davin Bellamy said. "First of all, we knew their defense couldn't stop our offense. We knew we were going to run right through them. We took them very lightly. We took them *very* lightly."

Mayfield was also better in person than he'd been on film. "He was a hell of a football player, a *hell* of a football player," Bellamy said. "We thought he would be timid because he never played a d-line like us, big and fast. He wasn't."

Georgia defenders hit Mayfield and talked trash to him, but he'd get right back up, talk trash back, and make another great play. He was carving Georgia up one first down after another.

The venue and magnitude of the game were also playing a role. This was the one time, Bellamy remembered later, that he was awed by his surroundings. That wasn't the case in South Bend or at the SEC Championship Game. But being at the Rose Bowl with a trip to the national championship at stake was different.

On the sideline Jonathan Ledbetter looked at nose tackle John Atkins. "Bro, we're playing with heart, but this ain't enough," Ledbetter said. "We gotta give everything we got or it's all over."

They would do that, but they would also need some luck. The ball literally bounced Georgia's way, but then someone—perhaps the 85th man on the 85-man roster—made the biggest play of his life and one of the most important plays of that season. Tae Crowder, a heretofore little-known special teamer, third-string inside linebacker, and former two-star recruit, may have made the most important play of the season. After taking the 31–14 lead in the waning seconds of the half, Oklahoma tried a squib kick on the kickoff. But it went right at Crowder, who not only had the dexterity to grab the ball, but also the awareness to hit the ground. That preserved five seconds. Georgia had the ball at the Oklahoma 47.

That was too long to try a field goal, but Kirby Smart thought they could run a quick play to get a few yards and still leave time on the clock. So that was the plan. There was only problem. Jim Chaney wasn't in the press box anymore. He was already in the elevator and headed down to the locker room for halftime. So Georgia coaches quickly huddled. James Coley suggested the play: an out pattern to Terry Godwin on the right sideline. It worked. Jake Fromm hit Godwin as he got out of bounds at the 38 with one second still left on the clock. It was another important catch that season for Godwin, who also caught the critical touchdown at Notre Dame. "Terry had a very quiet impactful career," Bellamy said. "Terry came through a lot on third downs."

And first downs after squib-kickoff recoveries. But it still left Rodrigo Blankenship a very long field goal of 55 yards, which would be a career long. But he made it. Georgia's deficit was now a manageable 14 heading into halftime. It was only three points in a game that had already seen plenty of scoring, but it gave the Bulldogs some life.

The sequence at the end of the first half and its series of improbable and comical events went down in program folklore. As they walked off, Shane Beamer said he "felt like the momentum had flipped a little bit. But there was also the reality that we've had a hard time slowing these guys down from Oklahoma for the last 30 minutes."

Smart came in the locker room and met in the small coaches' room with his staff. He was upbeat. He told the offensive coaches to get together and make sure they had a good plan for the second half but that they were doing a good job. As for the defense..."We're going to be okay," Smart told the staff. "We're going to simplify things and we're going to settle things down and be okay."

But when Smart went out to talk to the players, he had a different tone. Speaking to the team in the locker room, Smart challenged his players in a way Ledbetter hadn't heard Smart challenge them before. "[If] y'all want to lose this game, lose it. Lose it!" Smart said. "If you don't, go out there and make something happen for each other. Do it for each other."

Players recalled the locker room wasn't panicked in part because of how the first half ended but also because that was always the approach. "Athletically, man-to-man, we were so much stronger," Jeb Blazevich said. "We were just getting outschemed and outplayed."

Recalled Bellamy: "We knew that with the defense we've got, talent-wise they don't match up with us. Right now, they're just out-playing us. Let's just relax, go back out there, and do what you do. That was the message. Everybody calm down. They're not stopping our offense. Nobody panicked. Nobody argued."

Sony Michel also took control of the situation in the spacious locker room. First he went over to the defense. He told them: "I got your back!" Then Michel turned to the offense.

He repeated: "I got your back!"

Everybody was ready. They were back in what players called the "flow zone," where you don't think about it and just perform.

Georgia's offense got the ball first and scored on a Nick Chubb 50-yard run, continuing the momentum swing. It was a one-score game again. Then came the Georgia defense, which had tweaked its gameplan at halftime. After using more of a zone pass rush in the first half, they switched to what they called a "mush rush," where they rushed more man-to-man, didn't try too hard to get past the blocker, and tried to form a pocket around Mayfield to force him to backpedal.

Oklahoma did not score in the third quarter, and Georgia's defense went back to doing what it had all season. The rest of the game was a blur. Michel would make a play, and then Chubb would make a play. The defense would make a play. Georgia was soon ahead and seemingly in control, but Oklahoma's offense finally woke up and tied it with 8:47 left.

Then came the potential game-turner. Michel fumbled, and Oklahoma returned it 46 yards for a touchdown. Georgia trailed by seven with 6:52 left. But Georgia's player-led leadership kicked in. "Then immediately all of us were going around saying, 'Hey, get back into it, get everybody's mind right, and keep talking that truth that we knew. We know what to expect. We know what we're doing,'" Blazevich said.

Georgia moved downfield steadily, and when Chubb scored on a two-yard run and Blankenship's extra point tied it, there were only

55 seconds left. Pretty soon everyone had a chance to take a collective breath. The physical part of the game was one thing, but the emotional part was more exhausting. Going from the low of being down 31–14 to the high of taking the lead to the low of Michel's fumble, it was all back to square one with seemingly everything on the line. "Back and forth, back and forth, back and forth," Davis said. "We make a big play, and then they get a turnover, or then they hit a big play, and we get a turnover. Things happen so fast, and then we're in overtime."

Georgia got the ball first and went nowhere with two runs and an incompletion. But Blankenship earned his scholarship for the thousandth time that season—and not the last—by making a 38-yard field goal.

Oklahoma took the field and needed only a touchdown to win. "You're thinking: *Don't mess up. Don't mess up,*" Bellamy said. "That overtime moment, man, you really saw our team just like…had that championship mentality. We weren't going to lose that game. We were stopping them on third and [2]. Everything we practiced for is right here."

Georgia's defense made the stop and forced the field goal, which led to double overtime.

Oklahoma got the ball first this time, and after a gift from Georgia—an offside penalty—to give the Sooners first down at Georgia's 15, it tried a trick play.

Kyler Murray, the backup Oklahoma quarterback, was sent into the game to run the option. It was to Bellamy's side, and the Georgia veteran saw it coming. Murray was only coming into the game for one reason. Bellamy chased him and forced him out of bounds for no gain. Two plays later Oklahoma settled for another field goal try. Lined up over the middle of the line, Lorenzo Carter reached his arm up and blocked it. Zero points for the Sooners.

Georgia's offense then took the field. Throughout overtime Bellamy said players had been telling each other "one play away" over and over. Then it was entirely true. The first play lost two yards. The next play, however, is now shown on most every important Georgia highlight reel, including before every home game. The coaches later said they didn't give the play call much special thought. It had been called plenty of times already that season. Michel lined up in the Wildcat, took the direct snap, and ran to the left. There were some defenders on that side, but they were also blocked. Michel ran straight through them, down the sideline, and into history.

Georgia had won the Rose Bowl and was going to the national championship.

* * *

In the minutes after the game, Davin Bellamy had his viral moment. It all started when the teams arrived in Los Angeles, and Baker Mayfield got off the bus holding a sign that said "pretender." Mayfield was actually trolling ESPN announcer Lee Corso and the general notion that the Sooners didn't belong. But when some Georgia players saw it, they thought it was aimed at them. The next week Mayfield, who had the flu, did not attend a number of bowl events. So there wasn't any chance for interaction between the Heisman Trophy quarterback and the Bulldogs. They were slowly forming a perception of Mayfield, which would be reinforced the day of the game.

During pregame warm-ups Mayfield was working out by himself. Georgia receivers were also warming up on the sideline. As they were running routes, Mayfield's path along the sideline took him across midfield, and he went across the Georgia receivers, colliding with Terry Godwin. There was no grand confrontation, but there were some words exchanged. But the incident, if that's what you can call it, quickly made its way around the team.

Looking back years later, Bellamy now believes Mayfield was doing it intentionally to get in the heads of Georgia players. And it worked. "We wanted to hurt him instead of coming out and playing football. We just wanted to kill him," Bellamy said.

As Mayfield carved up Georgia's defense, he stared at the Bulldogs' sideline and threw in some trash talking as well. By the time the game ended, Bellamy decided it was time to get the last word in. "Humble yourself" just came out of his mouth. Those were the two words that were caught by the cameras and blown up on social media. He actually said: "Humble yourself at all times. If you don't, God will."

Other players just celebrated amongst themselves. Roses were passed out, and Godwin and others posed for pictures with the roses between their teeth. An exhausted Jonathan Ledbetter fell to the ground in the end zone right near when Michel had scored the winning touchdown. "We celebrated together," Ledbetter said. "We had fun on the field, we had fun on the stage, we had fun in the locker room. You've got guys tearing up, tears of joy for each other. They were just proud of each other. That was one of the most powerful moments of my life."

After the game Kirby Smart stepped on a chair in the middle of the room as he always does. They had just won a monumental game in stirring fashion. So, of course, Smart was going to ream into them. "Let me tell you something: we're not celebrating! There'll be plenty of time to celebrate this!" he said. "I want you guys in the shower, dressed, on that bus, on that plane back home, off your feet into bed. We've got another big game to play next week." Then he added: "Now, do you guys believe that I know what I'm talking about!"

Everybody knew what he meant. That's where Smart's background at Alabama and in playoff games gave him credibility.

The horde of media members was just outside the locker room, waiting to go in, when the door opened. Smart was leading a couple players to the press conference when he spied the media and yelled out to nobody in particular: "C'mon, we've got to get on a plane. These guys have got to get their sleep."

ARON DAVIS SLEPT ON THE PLANE RIDE HOME FROM Los Angeles. He doesn't remember watching the other semi-final. He was too exhausted to care. "I just kinda found out when we landed," he said.

The same went for many other players, including Jeb Blazevich. They had access to Wi-Fi on the plane, but many passed. "Honestly, I just needed to take a break. We just needed to hang out a second and take a breath," Blazevich said. "And it was really about being able to enjoy the moment before the next one had to happen."

Many of the coaches whipped out their iPads as the plane took off, already starting to prepare for the championship. Shane Beamer, however, had already done a lot of work that month on both Clemson and Alabama just in case, so he tried—unsuccessfully—to sleep. He ended up watching a movie to pass the time.

Georgia's plane was in the air when Alabama won. Nobody remembers how they found out. But by the time the plane took off, Alabama was already ahead, confirming most people's suspicions about what would happen anyway. So it was anticlimactic. Nobody was surprised, and everybody was happy about it. "We wanted Bama," Davin Bellamy said.

There was a psychological reason for that: the competitive desire to beat the best, the team they were measured against. But there was also a tangible football reason: the Georgia defense didn't want to have to prepare for Clemson's offense. That would require a week of practice for that spread offense after spending a month preparing for Oklahoma's different version of the spread. More headaches, more film work, and more confusion would have ensued.

Alabama, on the other hand, was just a carbon copy of Georgia. It would be like going against the first-team Georgia offense in practice. It was the ideal scenario for Georgia. "We already knew it was gonna be Alabama. We knew they were going to win out," Jonathan Ledbetter said. "We expected to play them. And to be honest, Coach Smart said we'd probably end up seeing them anyway."

On the outside it made for great storylines: Saban vs. Smart; teacher vs. protégé; Pruitt vs. Georgia, the team that he had recruited for and coached for less than two years ago; two teams from the same conference, playing in Georgia's backyard. But within Georgia's locker room, nobody really latched on to the outside narratives. That was a byproduct of the culture Smart instilled and modeled after the one Nick Saban had instilled at Alabama.

There was so much overlap between the two programs, so much potential emotion. Beamer was one of the few who could look at it with clear eyes, having never coached at Alabama and having joined Georgia only two seasons prior. He looked around and couldn't really sense anything extra among Smart, Mel Tucker, Glenn Schumann, and the players that week as they prepared for the Crimson Tide. "The familiarity certainly helped," Beamer said. "Knowing the players on Alabama's offense, defense, and special teams. Strengths and weaknesses, things like that. Kirby having so much familiarity with the Alabama defense, and their system and structure, things that maybe gave it trouble, and things that we could try to attack."

But extra emotion? Nah. The fact it was the national championship was enough. "I didn't really sense a big difference in our players other than the fact what you're playing for," Beamer said. "It was all business. Our schedule and our structure that week was no different than it had been any week all season."

They arrived back in the wee hours of the morning with a few signing the plane—it was the last time it was used—and then bussed back to the Butts-Mehre building, where some Georgia fans were waiting for them despite the hour. Most players were in bed by 7:00 AM—but only for a few hours. They still had to lift and run.

The rest of the schedule worked out perfectly. It was a Tuesday, but it felt like a Sunday given the game they had just played. And the team handled it like a Sunday since the national championship was exactly a week after the Rose Bowl. And the travel was almost non-existent. The national championship was at Mercedes-Benz Stadium in Atlanta. The good fortune continued.

The Bulldogs had the luxury of holing up in Athens, practicing as if it was just any other game. There were very few obligations of the sort they'd had in Los Angeles. The entire team and staff had to do a Media Day two days before the game, but they were in and out within an hour. They spent Saturday and Sunday in Atlanta at the hotel and doing a walk-through. It was seemingly back to normal—even if it wasn't. "After a crazy week in L.A., you're back there and like, *Aw man. Back to football!*" Blazevich said, laughing. "But we needed it. And we knew we needed it because we didn't have extra weeks to prepare."

Blazevich compared it to people at the end of a 400-meter race who were gassed and just giving what little they have left. That's how the team felt as they prepared for the 15th game of the season.

* * *

President Trump announced he would attend the game, which resulted in one of the more humorous—some would say telling—stories about Kirby Smart or football coaches in general.

Smart had visited the White House after Alabama won it all during the Obama administration. And during one of those visits, he had encountered a Secret Service agent who confessed to being a big Alabama fan.

Now Smart was with Georgia, which would have a walk-through at the stadium on Sunday, the day before the game. When Smart found out that Secret Service people would also be there that day doing advance work, he wanted to find out exactly which Secret Service members were going to be there. Would the big Alabama fan be among them? "You don't take any chances in a situation like that," Shane Beamer said, chuckling.

The president making an appearance showed the magnitude of the game, and that started to hit the team when it arrived for the game. It could have had the feel of an SEC Championship Game, considering the venue and the two teams. But the subtle differences cropped up: the national championship logos around the stadium, the heightened amount of media—more than had been even at the Rose Bowl—and the presence of all the security because of the president's visit. "The atmosphere, the energy in the dome that night was like very few things I'd ever been a part of," Beamer said. "You're trying to make it as normal as possible for your players, and knowing they're going to be extremely nervous, and have a lot of anxious energy, and try to get them through it. You realize what you're a part of and the excitement of it, but you also have a job to do."

It was quite a night for the Beamer family. Shane's father, Frank, was an inductee to the College Football Hall of Fame, so he was among those honored before the game and was present at the coin toss.

As the game approached, there was a calm in Georgia's locker room. They knew they were prepared. They felt cautiously confident. They knew the field. They looked around and knew the surroundings, the locker room. When they looked around, the only thing that was different was the realization that this would be their final game together. Everyone would go their separate ways the next day.

Georgia got the ball first. It did not begin well. Jim Chaney called three straight passes. The last one was picked off, but at least it was downfield in Alabama territory. Behind quarterback Jalen Hurts, the Crimson Tide drove down to Georgia's 17, but the drive stalled. Hurts rushed a pass on third down, and then Alabama missed what should have been an easy field goal. It would not be Alabama's last missed field goal.

Strangely, Chaney dialed up four more passes on the next drive, resulting in a 14-yard completion but then three straight incompletions. Cameron Nizialek came on to punt. Nick Chubb had yet to rush the ball, and Sony Michel had yet to touch it at all.

But everything began to turn from there. Georgia's defense forced a three-and-out. Chaney went to the run, giving it to Chubb or Michel on six straight plays. And when it looked like the drive had been snuffed out on a sack, Chaney called a surprise handoff to Michel on third and 20, which went for 26 yards. Four plays later Rodrigo Blankenship nailed a 41-yard field goal.

The rest of the half was a slow demolition by Georgia, which beat Alabama at its own game. Georgia put together a 13-play, 70-yard drive to lead to another field goal. Then it capped the half with a nine-play, 69-yard drive that finished with a Mecole Hardman one-yard touchdown run. Alabama's offense, meanwhile, could do nothing. Hurts struggled in that first half for the same reason Georgia had been able to shut down Notre Dame quarterback Brandon Wimbush way back in Week 2. Georgia's defense excelled at containing the outside run. Hurts couldn't get outside to run or to create more time to find an open receiver. Davin Bellamy, Lorenzo Carter, Roquan Smith, Aaron Davis, and the defense were doing their thing.

Bellamy remembers seeing Alabama players hanging their heads with helmets in their hands. They looked demoralized. There was one play on special teams when Bellamy hit someone, looked demoralized over him, and trash talked, and there was no response. *Oh yeah, y'all are done*, Bellamy remembered thinking.

It was Georgia 13, Alabama 0. Everything was set up for Georgia. But everything was about to change.

* * *

Georgia coaches ran down the tunnel, into the locker room, and, as they always did at halftime, into the smaller coaches' meeting room so they could quickly go over things before addressing the team. The room was the second door to the right at Mercedes-Benz Stadium. Kirby Smart looked at his coaches. "Listen to me," Smart said. "He's getting ready to make a quarterback change. Tua's coming in the game."

That seemed a stretch to some of the people in the room, including Shane Beamer. Jalen Hurts may have struggled in the first half, but he had led Alabama to that point. Tua Tagovailoa was only a freshman and had never started a game. Why would Nick Saban do that?

But Smart knew how Saban thought. So the coaches went into the main locker room, and the defense was warned not to be shocked to see No. 13 go in the game. There were nods of understanding. Aaron Davis said Georgia's defense had prepared for both quarterbacks. "We knew all about Tua and how special he was," Davis said. "So we said all week, 'We've got to prepare for both of these guys.'"

So perhaps Georgia was ready tactically. But looking back, Davin Bellamy blames himself for not being ready mentally. "For 14 games my message to the team was: we're not finished," he said. "Don't get too happy."

But not on January 8, 2018. "At halftime, man, I thought it was over," Bellamy said. "I thought it was over. And you've got to realize when you're a leader, you don't have to say it. People feed off your energy."

And his energy was saying that the game was in the bag. Apparently, others said it was all but over, too. "We all did," Jeb Blazevich said. "It was a lot harder to calm that excitement, and that might've went too far."

I was sitting in a front-row seat in the press box. At halftime I spoke with other writers, wondering what our next few days would be like. *Would there be a parade? Will we go to the White House to cover Georgia's visit?* Then I returned to my seat, and when the second half began—Alabama got the ball first—I could hear Cecil Hurt, the longtime scribe for *The Tuscaloosa News*, observe: "Number 13's in there."

There was a murmur in the crowd, too. At first the switch to Tagovailoa didn't work. Alabama went three and out and was sacked by Roquan Smith on third down. Then came the first of many what-might-have-beens for Georgia. Tyler Simmons, the former Alabama commit who followed Smart to Georgia, ran free and blocked Alabama's punt. It should have set up the Bulldogs for a kill shot deep in Alabama territory, but Simmons was called offside, as every Georgia fan painfully knows, and as every Georgia fan knows, Simmons was not offside. (Simmons assumed he was until after the game when I showed him a replay on my phone. Simmons' eyes got wide, and he said nothing but shook his head. He was on his way to forever being a meme, thanks to the way the rest of the game played out.)

On Alabama's second drive of the half, Tagovailoa did his thing: he scrambled for a first down on third and 7. Then he completed four passes in a row—the last for a touchdown—to make it Georgia 13, Alabama 7. We had a game again.

Jake Fromm realized that, too, and did his part to answer. The freshman zipped about the prettiest deep ball you will see down the right sideline, where Mecole Hardman grabbed it and ran it in for an 80-yard touchdown to make it Georgia 20, Alabama 7.

But Georgia's mistakes ensued. After Deandre Baker picked off Tagovailoa to set up Georgia at the Alabama 39, Fromm rushed a pass and was picked off himself, and Alabama returned it to the Georgia 40. That led to an Alabama field goal.

Georgia's next drive reached down to the Alabama 38 before stalling. "The play-calling went from 'let's win the game' to 'let's not lose the game,'" Blazevich said. Jackson Harris, then a junior tight end, described it as "very conservative. Let's just hold on to this so we can win. You can't do that against Alabama."

At one point, according to Blazevich, Georgia ran the same run play—*Flip left right Ohio*—four times in a row. It hit big the first time for about 10 yards, but then they called it three more times. "I'm like, *What? Why?*" Blazevich said. "So it hit big, first down, then three and out. I'm like, *What are we doing? Why would you do that? I understand hit them again.* Then let's hit them with a variation. It was the same play four times in a row...But we were still ahead."

But not for long. Georgia's defense wasn't built to stop a pocket passer as lethal as Tagovailoa, especially one as fresh as he was at that point. Tagovailoa went to some run-pass options, but Alabama also switched to more hurry-up partly out of necessity because of the clock and partly because Oklahoma had used it well against Georgia the week before. Either way it resulted in getting Georgia's defense off-balance. It was Tagovailoa's show. There were slants and swing throws on RPOs and just plain good pocket passes. That opened things up for the running game, too. And it took the edge rushers out of the same. "Me and Zo sacrificed a lot of sacks for scheme," Bellamy said. "You've got to be a disciplined player, very disciplined to sacrifice sacks for scheme. We knew Jalen Hurts didn't want to throw from the pocket, but we also knew these cats couldn't block us. Does that mean we're going to go do a spin move, get [off track], and give this dude all this space? No. We believed in the scheme, we believed it was going to work, and we contained rush."

That meant staying on the outside rather than rushing at the quarterback, thus preventing Hurts from scrambling. That was Georgia's scheme, and it worked against Brandon Wimbush at

Notre Dame, it worked in the second half against Baker Mayfield, and it worked to a tee in the first half against Hurts. But when Tagovailoa went in and was so good at throwing out of the pocket, that outside contain by Bellamy, Lorenzo Carter, and others opened up passing lanes over the middle of the field.

Alabama had thrown a curveball. Having tied it on a fourth-down pass on the previous drive, all seemed lost when Alabama got the ball with 2:50 left. Tagovailoa and the huge Alabama offensive line began a death march downfield. On the sideline Blazevich and offensive players felt helpless. Saban called for a quarterback kneel-down to set up a chip-shot field goal try with three seconds left, but then it missed. For a second straight week with everything on the line, Georgia would be playing in overtime.

This time, though, Blazevich wasn't sure the team was in the right frame of mind to win it. They had momentum back and said what they needed to say, but looking back, he thinks the emotion from the previous week was still catching up to Georgia while Alabama had coasted to a win in its playoff game. "We were just kinda...spent," he said.

It looked that way. Georgia's offense went three-and-out. Actually, it went backward. Fromm was sacked for a 13-yard loss on third down.

But Georgia still had Rodrigo Blankenship, who nailed a 51-yard field goal to make it Georgia 23, Alabama 20. Bellamy, Jonathan Ledbetter, and the rest of the Georgia first-team defense then took the field. They were about to experience an unimaginable range of emotions on two straight plays.

Tagovailoa dropped back on first down. And Ledbetter and Bellamy dropped back on him. Ledbetter got to him first but missed, but Bellamy was right there to bring him down. The same feeling ensued. Everything went quiet. Then came a sack and ecstasy. Except this time—unlike at Notre Dame and unlike the SEC Championship Game—the ball didn't come loose. Alabama still had second down.

But it seemed so unlikely in those brief seconds. There were 26 yards to go just for a first down! The chances for a game-tying field goal were even lower. "That kicker's confidence is *shot*," Bellamy said. "Nick Saban has ripped him on the sideline. Second and 26. I doubt he can come in here and hit a 50-yarder. I thought it was over."

He wasn't the only one. Shane Beamer had switched his mind from tight ends coach to special teams coordinator, getting ready for his field goal block team in case it came to that.

"It's second and 26. You realize they've got a field-goal kicker who's struggling," Beamer said. "They've got three plays left, but you realize you're in great position to win the national championship."

The head coach, meanwhile, was thinking about the very next play. And once again he had a premonition. As soon as Bellamy brought Tagovailoa to the ground, Smart yelled into his headset: "They're gonna take a shot here."

Once again Smart's intuition about his former team was right.

Davis recalled something else that hurt Georgia's defense on the play. Normally before a long down-and-distance play, the Georgia defense would sub in its dime package and get an extra defensive back out there. But Georgia was still in nickel, even though it took Alabama 30 seconds to run the next play. "We tried to call something a little safe to try to protect ourselves," Davis said, "because we knew they were going to need a big chunk play to get the first down."

Watching on the sideline, Blazevich got a weird feeling. That feeling usually meant something great was about to happen —a turnover to win the game—or something bad. Second down began. Tagovailoa again dropped back to pass. And everyone knows what happened really.

Davis re-routed his receiver and then looked back at the quarterback. "I just see the ball launched in the air and I'm just tracking it and I see the Alabama receiver fall underneath it," Davis said. "It was disbelief at that moment. I almost didn't want to accept it that this is how the game ended."

Bellamy had rushed the quarterback again and came inside. He believes now he only needed an eighth of a second more to hit Tagovailoa to stop the pass from getting off. Instead Bellamy saw the pass go out and then looked up and behind him. "As soon as I saw the guy running wide open, I knew it was over," Bellamy said.

On the sideline Blazevich's premonition was coming true. "As soon as he threw the ball, I knew it. This isn't good," Blazevich said. "It's over."

Beamer watched helplessly on the sideline. You can be a veteran coach who has been through painful finishes and gut-wrenching losses, but nothing prepares you for this. He was standing by himself as it all happened. "It was almost like it was slow motion," Beamer said. "I remember him just dropping back, throwing that ball, and it seems weird, but it literally seemed like everything slowed down. And you realize this guy's open. And unless he drops it, he's probably about to catch this thing for a touchdown. And then he caught it. And to be honest after that, I don't remember anything after that. It was a feeling I never want to experience again."

Alabama freshman receiver DeVonta Smith, who had once been committed to Georgia, had run free down the left sideline. Georgia cornerback Malkom Parrish had let Smith go by because Georgia was in Cover-2. Safety Dominick Sanders, who had that side of the field, wasn't there either. For all of his youth, Tagovailoa eye-faked to the other side of the field, and Sanders had briefly bought it for only a critical moment. Smith hauled in the touchdown pass. And it was over.

Beamer walked around in a daze, shaking hands. But in his mind, it was impossible to not replay what just happened—not just the second-and-26 play but some of the plays that had turned the game from Tyler Simmons to Tagovailoa's seemingly impossible throws.

The reaction of Georgia fans may have been best summed up by one that was caught on live television. Mike Bobo, who was analyzing the game along with other coaches on an ESPN show, put his hands on his head in disbelief when Alabama scored, sighed, and could say nothing. Smart had the most measured reaction. The ESPN camera on Smart showed him watching the flight of the ball and then immediately taking his headset off, turning to look ahead, and walking to the center of the field to find Saban.

The mentor and protégé embraced briefly. Smart shook his head at him, tacitly acknowledging what an unbelievable game it was. There were Georgia players standing around stunned, especially on the sideline. The locker room was pretty quiet. Everyone was still in shock. There were a few angry players. There wasn't much time to process in the locker room because the cooling-off period before the media came in was seemingly too brief. There was anger, self-doubt, and a helpless feeling because the season—and in some cases, like for Blazevich, their football career—was over. "You're like: *hold on, this isn't how the story ends*," Blazevich said.

Even for the players with more football to play, there was still a realization of what had been lost. "It's like a big shock. You sat there and said: 'This really happened,'" Harris said. "You had such a high and then you're at such a low. It's like, *Did I just dream that?*"

Smart spoke to the team, mustering a few words about understanding the pain of the loss, the need to stay together and work through it, and a message of thanks to the seniors for what they had done for the team. But there was only so much he could say. Grown men were crying. Some remained in stunned silence. Some were trying to contain their anger. "I've been in a lot of locker rooms after a loss," Beamer said. "Never in my career have I ever been in one as emotional and painful as that one was. That's something I'll never get over."

Beamer walked into the coaches' locker room. It was silent. Nobody was talking. Someone walked in and let Beamer know that his parents were outside and wanted to know if he wanted to talk. So Shane Beamer walked out and met them. He doesn't remember what he or his father said. "I was still in a daze at that point," he said. "There wasn't much to say."

When the media came in the locker room, some players got out of there as fast as they could. Carter, who had taken the Auburn game so hard, couldn't bear to be out there. He stayed in the showers, as did Sanders and Parrish. They weren't the only ones. Nick Chubb, Sony Michel, and others spoke reluctantly. Fromm stood outside his locker and did his best. It had been the longest season in any of these players' lives and it had finished in the most heartbreaking fashion on the largest stage in college football. "Understanding that with this thing that we do, we're going to have to face the media, and somebody has to be the one to go talk to them," Davis said, "and reassure our fans and our players that we're still okay. It hurts. It hurts bad, but you live to see tomorrow. That shows how the seniors were able to step up and make some sense out of some things that happened."

Bellamy was among those who stood at his locker and patiently took all comers. "My message was: in the most important game of your life, the most important time of your life, the most important play of your life, you weren't focused," Bellamy said. "For 14 games you were focused. For the last play, you weren't focused. I didn't want to single guys out, but...focus. And that's what Coach Smart preached: focus. We let them off the hook."

Remembering the play more than a year later while sitting in a booth in a restaurant outside Atlanta, Bellamy again shook his head in disgust. There are athletes who often put up the veneer of quickly getting past defeats and moving forward. But players like Bellamy on that Georgia team had to learn to be able to move forward while also not getting past that one defeat. There was nothing cathartic about pretending to forget the most painful loss of their lives. It didn't take away from what the team had accomplished in a special season to acknowledge the regret and disbelief over the way it ended. "I'll never forget that one because I can never go back and play them again," Bellamy said more than a year later. "There's no re-dos. They won. It's like somebody sucker punched you in the face, then hopped on a plane, and you never saw them again."

The team had a breakfast the following morning at the hotel. The mood hadn't brightened at all. In fact, the feeling was perhaps worse because it was hitting everyone that it was really over. The season, the national championship hopes, and the college careers for so many important people were finished. Beamer looked around and saw Smith, who was likely to turn pro, and so many other guys that weren't just good players but people he enjoyed being around. This was the last time everyone on this team was going to be together. Then they got on the bus and headed back to Athens. "It's such a great year and just like that it's over," Beamer said.

The hurt made it hard for some to truly appreciate what happened over those months. It may be that time and distance is required for the players to truly understand how special that season ended up being. Kevin Butler won a national championship at Georgia. He won a Super Bowl with the Chicago Bears. Both were as a player. He was only a staff member on this Georgia team, but he didn't need long to know it ranked right up there with the magical seasons he had in the '80s. "That season was as much fun as any season I've ever been involved with," Butler said. "As a player, as a coach, going up to Notre Dame, and just the games and the way they played, and seeing the attitude and how hard they worked. I mean, that's where I can really say that and really mean it. People are like, 'Well, you were in a Super Bowl.' Yeah, I was in a Super Bowl, and we won it. But I understand that kind of commitment and the passion. Damn, Kirby's brought a true passion back to Georgia football."

16

Moving On

senior on that 2018 team. "So I think it takes a lot of leadership. You have to set the tone. You have to be with the team's leaders and steer the ship pretty well. And I think we did that pretty well."

The coaching staff, meanwhile, had to turn their attention fully to the future—and in some cases their own. Shane Beamer, who had helped put together the special teams and offensive gameplan in the Rose Bowl, was about to switch sides. Oklahoma head coach Lincoln Riley called Beamer about a job on his staff, offering a role in the offense and the title of associate head coach. There was also a raise. Beamer took the offer to Kirby Smart, but both seemed to know the way it would go. Smart thanked Beamer for his two seasons, Beamer thanked Smart for the opportunity, and Beamer was off.

While Beamer's departure took away a longtime friend from his staff, it gave Smart an opportunity. In the run-up to the playoffs the previous month, new Texas A&M head coach Jimbo Fisher had come calling for receivers coach James Coley. The two had worked together at Florida State and LSU, and Fisher, while he would be calling plays for the Aggies, could offer Coley the title of offensive coordinator and a raise. From a career and status standpoint, it seemed a no-brainer for Coley. He should go to Texas A&M. But Coley and his family also liked Athens. His kids played basketball in the YMCA league, where I would see Coley simultaneously watching his son and also making recruiting calls and texts. Coley was from a family of Cuban immigrants, so he was used to adapting, but he also wasn't desperate to leave. And Smart wasn't eager for Coley, one of Georgia's best recruiters, to depart either.

Smart offered a counterproposal. He would match or even top the financial offer from Texas A&M. That was no problem. The problem was that he couldn't offer Coley the full offensive coordinator job. Jim Chaney still needed to have that. But Smart could give Coley the title of co-offensive coordinator, which would come with some more responsibilities like sitting next to Chaney in the press box during games, helping call plays. But most important of all, Coley could switch from coaching receivers to quarterbacks. That was not an out-of-nowhere proposition. Coley had coached quarterbacks most of his career, including at Miami, before switching to receivers in order to latch on to Smart's staff at Georgia. But Coley was ecstatic to return to coaching quarterbacks and accepted Smart's offer.

The only problem now for Smart was that Chaney had also been the quarterbacks coach for most of his career. It's what had he had come to Georgia to do. He would not be happy with being taken off the role. But Smart's decision was final. He placed a lot of value in the recruiting column, and Coley's recruiting was simply better than Chaney's. But when Beamer left, of course, it opened up the tight ends job. Smart took some time mulling everything over because the NCAA had also instituted a new rule allowing teams to have a 10th assistant coach. That allowed him to split Beamer's two roles. Chaney was moved to tight ends, a position he had coached in 2007 with the St. Louis Rams, and for the special teams coordinator role, Smart called up Scott Fountain, who had taken that job with Mississippi State a few weeks earlier but hadn't given up his place in Athens yet. Fountain ended up returning and getting a raise. (Fountain's service in 2017 as a special teams analyst had proved invaluable.)

There was also an opening to fill on the defensive side. Kevin Sherrer, the last holdover from the Mark Richt era, at least on the assistant coaching staff, left to re-join Jeremy Pruitt at Tennessee. Once again, Smart reached back to his Alabama days and hired Dan Lanning, who was a linebackers coach at Memphis but had been at Alabama in an off-the-field role. Lanning was young, energetic, and —always the most attractive attribute to Smart—a strong recruiter.

There were other small changes on Smart's staff. Kevin Butler's time as a student assistant was up. Aaron Feld, the telegenic assistant strength coach, got the head strength job at Oregon. Other quality control staffers and graduate assistants moved on to bigger roles elsewhere. Other additions included Smart's old friend,

Tyson Summers, who had been fired the previous fall as Georgia Southern's head coach, being brought on as a defensive analyst. (Summers actually joined the team in time for the playoff run and was in the coaching press box for the Rose Bowl.)

In the midst of all this, Smart had something else brewing. Although his team had not dethroned Alabama on the field, it was about to do so off the field and win the unofficial national recruiting championship. Most of the work had been done by mid-December. The advent of the early signing period saw a haul that featured a bevy of five-star prospects, including the nation's highest-ranked quarterback in Justin Fields, who had committed to much fanfare the previous October. Sam Pittman was also on a roll, not only reeling in five-star Jamaree Salyer from Atlanta (whom Clemson was after), but also five-star Cade Mays almost literally from Tennessee's own backyard. Mays was from Knoxville, Tennessee, and his father played for the Volunteers, and yet Pittman got him (In a later weird turn of events, of course, Mays still ended up going back to Tennessee after two years at Georgia.) Pittman also got the center of the future, Trey Hill. Running backs coach Dell McGee not only ran lead on Fields, but also pulled in five-star Zamir White from Laurinburg, North Carolina. (Georgia's rich history of tailbacks from North Carolina did not hurt.) With a lot of help from Mel Tucker, Coley teamed up to reach into south Florida for five-star cornerback Tyson Campbell, four-star tailback James Cook, and four-star cornerback Divaad Wilson.

In all, Georgia signed an astounding eight five-star recruits, which would have been impressive enough, but it also burnished the national recruiting strategy that Smart installed when he became coach. Georgia signed the top-rated players in six different states: Georgia, North Carolina, Florida, Tennessee, Illinois, and South Carolina. This was all the result of the buildup the past few years. Georgia held together most of that first, abbreviated class in 2016; got Jake Fromm, D'Andre Swift, and others for that No. 3-ranked 2017 class; and then took advantage of the program's improved on-field fortunes for the 2018 class. Whereas before the Georgia staff had been selling hope, playing time, and other possibilities, this time they could also point to the on-field results. "That was key," Rusty Mansell, a recruiting guru, said, "because other programs were starting to negatively recruit against Georgia and the coaching staff's ability to win. They couldn't say that anymore after that season."

Smart was also able to capitalize for his own financial benefit. But even then he and Jimmy Sexton were able to make sure it was about more than just money. Georgia's administration approached Smart about a new contract, an obvious move after such a magical second season. They eventually agreed on what amounted to an annual salary of $7 million, which went through 2024. That was the number that got most of the headlines. But buried near the end of the agreement was the more key number. Georgia agreed to guarantee Smart at 65 percent of the deal. Put another way: if Smart was let go at any time, he would be owed 65 percent of the remaining contract. Meanwhile, Smart would owe Georgia less than 50 percent if he left at any point under a structure that saw his guarantee gradually decrease as the years went on.

Sexton had negotiated similar deals for his clients. Jimbo Fisher had a 100 percent guarantee from Texas A&M on his gargantuan contract ($75 million over 10 years), and Gus Malzahn had a 75 percent guarantee on his contract, which was similar to Smart's in salary and length. The higher the guarantee, the more leverage a coach had. And Sexton and Smart valued that at Georgia, knowing that Mark Richt had been undone by not using leverage when he had the opportunity. The result was Georgia falling behind in facilities and spending. Smart would make sure that didn't happen under his watch.

In fact, during the summer of 2018, Georgia opened the newest, glitziest part of its facilities rebuild: the recruiting lounge, which was more like a giant ballroom, and new locker rooms at Sanford Stadium. It was part of a $63 million upgrade. The team had been using the same decrepit locker room that Smart used as a player.

The project was in the works before Smart arrived, but he would benefit from it. And almost as soon as it was opened, Smart was getting ready for the next project: a new football facility with meeting rooms, offices, and a new weight room. That was also badly needed, especially with Smart adding more staff—some staffers were sharing offices or working out of cramped rooms—and the weight room had long since fallen behind that of SEC competitors.

The new football facility was not greenlit until well into 2019. But if the slow approach bothered Smart, he was still careful to say otherwise in public. In fact, when athletic director Greg McGarity received a one-year contract extension early in 2019, Smart released a statement praising McGarity in part for his work with facilities. Richt and others would have guffawed at the statement. But Smart knew the right approach to take.

As Smart continued to win—in games and recruiting—he also began to consolidate more power. The responsibility for non-conference scheduling was shifted to the football office, where Smart and Josh Lee, the football operations director, worked in tandem. Smart wanted to think big with his non-conference scheduling. And he trusted Lee, a point man, for making the games happen and to do his best to fit them in the schedule as best as possible (as in go play Florida State a week after playing Kentucky rather than, say, Auburn.)

There were changes afoot everywhere, and despite the pain of how the national championship had ended, the feelings around the program were as good as they had ever been. Georgia seemed to sign every recruit it went after. National pundits were saying that Smart was building a powerhouse that would sustain. The fanbase was happy. The administration was happy. The rest of the SEC had a new and grudging respect for Smart and Georgia. But Smart also knew that what they had accomplished in Year Two had set the tone for something else the next few years. Nothing again would be easy.

17

Jake Fromm
and Justin Fields

F OR ALL THE TALENT COMING INTO GEORGIA'S PROGRAM and for all the great feelings around the program, in hindsight the expectations should have been lowered for the 2018 season. There was too much talent—and more importantly, veteran leadership—that had walked out the door at pretty much every position: Nick Chubb and Sony Michel in the backfield, Isaiah Wynn on the offensive line, Jeb Blazevich and Javon Wims at tight end and receiver, Lorenzo Carter and Davin Bellamy at outside linebacker, Doninick Sanders and Aaron Davis in the secondary, John Atkins on the defensive line, and Roquan Smith at inside linebacker.

Taking his decision until nearly the last minute, Smith turned pro the day of the NFL early entrant deadline. A loyal and happy teammate to the end, Smith said his heart made him want to stay for his senior year. But his head won out, as did the many in his ear telling him it would be a silly decision to stick around when he was almost certain to be a high first-round pick. And he was taken by the Chicago Bears eighth overall.

Deandre Baker, who had a great junior season at cornerback, also took his decision to the deadline but opted to stay another year. He would say later he decided once and for all while watching ESPN on deadline day, and the second-and-26 highlight came on. Baker, who was on the other side of the field when the play happened, wanted to make sure that would never happen again. But Baker was not quite the leader that Smith—or even Sanders or Davis—was. It was a huge positive for Georgia's defense to have Baker in 2018, and he went on to become a consensus All-American and first-round pick. But Baker also came to symbolize what Georgia had lacked in this team. He was a quiet guy, a contrast to the take-charge leaders of the 2017 team.

In their follow-up act to their special season, the Georgia Bulldogs went from a player-led locker room full of accountability to a quieter one occasionally with different agendas, where the best and most vocal leaders didn't tend to be playing that much. It left Kirby Smart and his staff frustrated at times—not so much because it was a huge problem, but it compared so unfavorably to what the team had been like the year before.

Jake Fromm was at least back to lead the offense, as was Andrew Thomas on the offensive line and D'Andre Swift in the backfield. They were also only sophomores. Center Lamont Gaillard, a fifth-year senior, was appointed another leader, but like Baker he was a more of laid-back type. There were also elite-level players ready to break out—namely receivers Mecole Hardman and Riley Ridley at receiver. And forgotten in the backfield his first two years, Elijah Holyfield was ready to step into a bigger role.

It was a mix of talent and personalities that had the potential to do a lot on the field and be combustible off it. And into the mix was introduced a player and a situation that proved to overshadow the team throughout the year.

Justin Fields was one of the nation's top prospects and a quarterback with tantalizing dual-threat running and throwing abilities. He was also in Georgia's proverbial backyard, Harrison High School in Kennesaw, Georgia, about 80 minutes from Athens' campus. But as of the summer of 2017—around the time Jacob Eason was expected to be Georgia's starter and Fromm his backup—Fields was committed to Penn State. Georgia was also in heavy pursuit of another in-state quarterback, Trevor Lawrence of Cartersville. Smart knew that Georgia had let another in-state quarterback get away to Clemson, and Deshaun Watson had made his home-state team eternally regret it. Smart didn't want that to happen again.

But as Lawrence's recruiting process went along, it became clear he would be going to Clemson. Smart kept trying, even making his first visit of a recruiting period to Lawrence. (Why not? It wasn't far away.) But soon it became apparent this was going to be a losing battle, a rare thing for Smart on the recruiting trail these days. So they had to adjust.

Enter Fields.

His skillset would not normally fit in with Georgia's offense, but when the Fields family and Georgia coaches met, they found a potential match. Fields didn't want to be pigeonholed as a running quarterback and wanted to play in a pro-style offense. And with his Alabama defense once burned by Watson in the national championship game, Smart wanted a dual-threat quarterback. Both sides were sure they could make it work. Fields soon de-committed from Penn State and committed to Georgia on the afternoon of Friday, October 6, during a ceremony at his high school. Such was the attention and excitement that Atlanta television station FOX 5 flew a helicopter over Harrison High School to try to capture the moment.

A day later, when Georgia won easily at Vanderbilt, another FOX 5 reporter almost dropped their microphone while placing it in front of Smart's podium. "I thought you guys were over Harrison?" Smart said with a sly smile. Reporters laughed.

Everybody felt great about the commitment, at least outwardly. Yes, there could be worries about having a quarterback controversy. But Smart repeated the term "quarterback competition," and that became the catchphrase. As the season went on, it became apparent that Eason wouldn't have to deal with Fields because he'd be transferring. That left only Fromm and Fields, and, of course, any team wanted a talented backup option—perhaps even legitimate competition for the starting job. Fields was considered to be that good.

But there were only a few scant times he would show that skill at Georgia. There was the spring game, when Fields threw a few nice deep balls. The potential was evident in practices and scrimmages as well, but there were also signs that the situation was just not comfortable. Fromm had built up a lot of support in the locker room. He had personally helped recruit many of the members of his 2017 class and had an outgoing and hard-working personality that endeared him to veterans. And even with Eason gone, there was no sense that Fromm would let up. Players did understand why Fields was brought in; he was a great recruit, and what if something happened to Fromm?

But Fields didn't come to Georgia to sit. He did genuinely love the school, the team, and Smart. But he also had his future in mind and was confident enough in his abilities that he thought he had a great chance to beat out Fromm. Put together a starting quarterback who had earned the right to keep his job, a great recruit with the ability and desire to take the job, and a coaching staff who wanted to keep them both happy and on campus, and you had a situation. Smart had to navigate it carefully.

Something stuck with me about Jim Chaney's body language when he gave his preseason press conference in 2018, and he was asked about Fields. Normally bubbly and loose, Chaney seemed to tighten up. He grabbed the podium with both hands and started to choose his words carefully. "We all know how polarizing the quarterback position can be," Chaney said.

The players, as they had been for several years now (even under Mark Richt), were under orders not to say much if anything about the quarterbacks. But it was noticeable that while they would praise Fields' talent, they would quickly turn to Fromm and continue to talk about him in near-reverential tones. This was where Georgia was in a good spot as far as avoiding the type of controversy that could tear a locker room apart. Fromm still had the support of the team.

The coaches tried to keep Fields happy by playing him, but it became unwieldy. He didn't get much of a chance to throw except for the end of blowouts. So when Fields was put in the game in package-type situations, including SEC games that were still in doubt, it was mainly as a runner. It wasn't what Fields had in mind. He wanted to throw. But Georgia also had games to win and, when it came to airing it out, it still had Fromm. In contrast to

Fromm, Fields was more of a quiet personality. He kept to himself a bit more. One player said privately that it was hard to get to know him. Maybe he would have come out of his shell more in future years at Georgia. We'll never know.

Whether it was the quarterback situation or the weight of expectations, it was apparent that the 2018 version of the Georgia football team was not quite picking up where the last team left off. The overall talent may have been just as good, but it was younger and unproven. The leadership was not emerging.

There was a noticeable difference in Smart's demeanor at press conferences. The year before he had been more loose. This year he was more tight, the way he had been at times in his first year. During the 2017 season, Smart had seemed to talk with a twinkle in his eye, almost a wink to the media that said, "Yeah, I know what we've got here. I just can't say it." But the 2018 version of the press conferences was back to frowned expressions and occasionally chippy responses.

Through it all, however, Georgia kept winning. Considering the way the previous season ended, it was arguably the best sign that Smart would sustain the program. Some of the scores were tighter than the previous year but not all of them. Georgia went into South Carolina the second week of the season and won going away. The trip to Missouri two weeks later was only in doubt near the end (if you considered a two-touchdown lead in doubt). That was followed by easy wins against Tennessee and Vanderbilt at home, and Georgia carried a 6–0 record into Baton Rouge, Louisiana, on October 13.

That's when the humbling came. It was also when Fromm had his worst game of the season, as again the coaches force-fed Fields into the game in a seemingly pointless manner.

Fromm and Fields alternated on several plays, but again Fields didn't throw a pass, so LSU's defense was able to guess pretty well what was coming. Perhaps better than the Georgia fans who couldn't figure out what their coaches were thinking. Fromm did throw 34 times, completing less than half of them, and was picked off twice.

There was also a very questionable call by Smart, which would be pointed to often—perhaps too much—as the reason for the way the game went south. Georgia was only trailing 3–0 late in the first quarter when its drive stalled at the LSU 14. Out came Rodrigo Blankenship for a seemingly chip-shot field goal, but Smart and special teams coordinator Scott Fountain had other ideas. They had seen a weakness in LSU's field goal coverage unit and thought the right side would be open for Blankenship to run. They planned to use the play at some point in the game and decided this was the time, even though Blankenship, who was not known for his running ability, would need to gain nine yards for the first down. The play was over before it really had a chance. To its credit, LSU snuffed it out well. Cornerback Greedy Williams never looked away from Blankenship and led the way in swarming him. The momentum was now completely on LSU's side.

The rest of the game was almost as painful for Georgia. During a brief spell in the fourth quarter, Georgia seemed to have a chance to still make it a game, but Fromm threw an interception. The play-calling didn't help. Chaney went away from a running game that early on was opening holes that Holyfield was running through to the second level. But even if Chaney had stuck with the run game, it may have only been a matter of time. LSU head coach Ed Orgeron later said that the Tigers had quickly adjusted their defensive front strategy, so those holes weren't going to open nearly as wide.

This ultimately was just not going to be Georgia's day—much like a year earlier it had not been in the cards for Georgia while playing at another SEC West opponent. The only question was whether, like last year, this was just a bump, or if the loss exposed a team with deeper problems. Smart privately may have had his worries that it was the latter—whether that was because of the run defense, the player leadership, or something else. But in his postgame statements he leaned on recent history. "This is very similar to last year," Smart said.

18

Alabama in Atlanta—Again

B EFORE THE 2018 SEASON BEGAN, JONATHAN LEDBETTER WAS standing on a balcony at an Atlanta hotel and turned to look at the big building—Mercedes-Benz Stadium—that loomed a few blocks away. It wasn't the first time he had been back since that night in early January. He spent a lot of time in Atlanta and passed by it all the time. "I never have regret," Ledbetter said. "I watched the game right after we played it. There's things we could have done differently. We could have changed the outcome of that game, but everything happens for a reason," he said. "You've got to keep pushing. You can't live in the past."

Whether or not the Georgia football team had privately moved past it, they had done a good job of seeming unaffected on the field. After falling flat at LSU in October, the Bulldogs had pulled things together and went on a roll, easily winning their second straight division title. That meant they would not have to wait to play Alabama. It would happen once again in that same building—this time in the SEC Championship Game.

The storylines were obvious. Many of the key players from the previous season were gone, but Tua Tagovailoa had cemented himself as Alabama's star. He entered the game as the favorite for the Heisman Trophy. The Crimson Tide were now an offensive juggernaut. The Bulldogs weren't too shabby either but still entered as a two-touchdown underdog. Most observers didn't expect them to be able to hang with an opposing offense that could seemingly score at will. This was not a mirror image matchup for Georgia, which was also a much younger team than the one that had gone toe to toe with mighty Alabama 11 months earlier. The thinking was that this time it would have to do everything right and then get some luck.

But once again events would not play out as anybody could have guessed. On the morning of the SEC Championship Game, Georgia was again getting ready to head over to Mercedes-Benz Stadium and play its nemesis, Alabama. The feeling this time, however, was different. It wasn't really that the stakes were different. Although this wasn't the national championship, it still felt like it to Georgia, which knew it almost certainly needed to win it to make the playoff while unbeaten Alabama was assured a spot with a loss. No, this time it was more about the journey. The previous year had been about an unexpected and joyful run at basically every point. The 2018 season had been about just meeting expectations. Georgia had done that, shaking off the LSU loss and romping to wins, including a de facto SEC East championship at Kentucky, an upstart team with upset hopes that the Bulldogs had dispensed with in relatively quick fashion.

Then came Alabama. Georgia players returned to the same locker room as the previous season, walked the same tunnels, and walked on the same field. The teams flipped sidelines from the national championship, but otherwise it felt the same. So meaningful in the previous season's game, Tyler Simmons was the first player out of Georgia's locker room for warm-ups. That wasn't intentional, but it was quite symbolic. Ledbetter and Elijah Holyfield were two of the captains. As they walked to midfield for the coin toss, holding their helmets under their arms, they were both trying to choke back tears. They remained confident even if Georgia was considered a massive underdog. "We believed in each other so much that we didn't care who didn't," Ledbetter said. "It was about us and it's always been about us."

Over the next two-plus hours, these Bulldogs showed that they had been underestimated. The defense crippled Tagovailoa —figuratively and almost literally—and knocked him to second place in the Heisman race. Jake Fromm and the offense went up and down the field, as Jim Chaney once again had put together a great gameplan, and the offense executed it well—at least for the next two-plus hours.

The high-water mark for Georgia came in the third quarter, when Fromm found Isaac Nauta over the middle for a long catch and run, and Nauta wasn't brought down until he was well in Alabama territory. It was easy field-goal range for the great Rodrigo Blankenship—at minimum—and perhaps more. Georgia already led 28–14, which seemed enough of a cushion as its defense stifled an Alabama offense that now didn't seem so vaunted. But when the drive stalled and Blankenship came out for a 31-yard field goal, he inexplicably missed. ("I just rushed it," Blankenship said after the game.) It was the same side of the field that Alabama's kicker had missed the chip shot that would have won last season's game in regulation. Maybe that was it. Who knows? All that was certain was that Alabama got a much-needed dose of momentum and hope.

Georgia's sideline—and considerable fanbase—got that familiar sense of *uh oh.*

Feeling better after twisting his ankle earlier in the game, Tagovailoa pounced, hitting on a 51-yard touchdown pass. Georgia's lead was already down to 28–21. Georgia's offense, meanwhile, started to go back in the tank, the same way it had on the same field at the same point against the same opponent 11 months earlier. Then came the plot twist.

Tagovailoa took a hit, went down, and this time couldn't come back in. The hit was administered by Ledbetter, who would later, knowing the result of his hit, put it this way: "I felt robbed. I personally felt robbed."

So Jalen Hurts, who had rested the whole game but had two years of starting experience, came in. It was the worst possible set-up for Georgia's defense. "We were exhausted," Ledbetter said. "He came in fresh. There's some things that I wish we could've done differently, but that's how the cards unfolded."

The previous season Georgia's defense was perfectly suited to stop the mobile Hurts because Davin Bellamy, Lorenzo Carter, and Roquan Smith were so good on the edge—not to mention Aaron Davis and

J.R. Reed. This time only Reed was back, and D'Andre Walker, who had emerged as an able replacement at outside linebacker, hurt his groin during the game. He was out, and Hurts was in. The backup Alabama quarterback proceeded to run all over Georgia's defense, extending plays with his feet and arm. Alabama tied it with 5:19 left.

Even then, Georgia's offense was able to move the ball. But that only set up a fateful decision that would be derided and debated for some time. This actually went back to the previous season. Georgia had a fake punt ready to go against Alabama in the national championship, having seen a weakness on film in the Crimson Tide's punt coverage unit. Smart also remembered a successful fake punt Georgia had used on Alabama in the 2012 SEC Championship Game. They put the fake in for the national championship, practiced it...but never pulled the trigger. "We were going to run it, but then we called out of it," Ledbetter said.

No one ever knew, which meant Georgia still had it in the bag to use this time. Kirby Smart wasn't going to hold off. Though much derided, the decision to do it when he did was actually the right call. The execution of it, however, could not have been more clumsy. Georgia had reached midfield, but the drive stalled with 3:04 left. It was fourth and 11. And the call was put in. Risky? Yes. Disastrous if it didn't work? Yes. But there was a good reason to try. It was the Bulldogs' only hope.

Sideline reporter Chuck Dowdle was watching it all unfold from up close. "Seeing the look on our kids' eyes as they were coming off the field, our defense, I felt like if we gave the ball back to Alabama, I don't care if it was at the 50 or the 150, Alabama was going to score again," Dowdle said. "I really felt out best chance to win that game was to somehow figure out a way to maintain that football."

But the play never had a chance because of how badly it was handled. First and most importantly, Justin Fields was the up-man. Alabama players noticed him right away. Fields had not been the up-man on any punt before. That was almost like announcing: *this is going to be a fake.* The Bulldogs also took too long to snap the ball. Perhaps with a quicker snap, not enough players would have noticed Fields, and the receiver would have been open. Even then, it would have required 11 yards, which was asking a lot. The call itself may have been inspired. Everything else about it was disastrous. Fields panicked and scrambled but was quickly enveloped, and Alabama got the ball at its own 48. "They did notice [Fields]. We took too long to get it set. We took too long to get the ball off," Ledbetter said. "But the funny thing about it is the year before if you had switched scenarios, the games would have switched, too. So [Smart] didn't call it in 2017. But he did call it in 2018. I'm not mad at him for that because I get it."

Hurts needed just five plays to move downfield and score the go-ahead touchdown. Georgia's offense did get the ball back with 1:04 left and reached the Alabama 39. But a Hail Mary—into the same end zone the national championship game had ended in—was incomplete. Once again, the confetti rained down on a victorious Alabama team—and a devastated Georgia squad. "This feels just like last year. Nothing different," Deandre Baker, Georgia's star corner-back, told me in the locker room afterward. Baker had stayed on the bench for several minutes after it ended, not moving. It was his last game in college. "They got away with it a second time," Baker said, shaking his head. "This is the second time they got away from us."

Smart went on ESPN that night and made an impassioned case for Georgia making the playoff anyway. He had his supporters, who thought that Georgia had clearly shown it was one of the four best teams in college football by hanging with mighty Alabama the way it had. But ultimately not enough members of the selection committee agreed. Georgia finished fifth in the voting—one slot behind Oklahoma. Georgia players and coaches knew it was a longshot. The committee was not going to put in a two-loss, non-champion over a one-loss conference champion. Players could only shake their heads and think about what if. "I know it's been quoted a thousand times. Coach Saban knows who he doesn't want in the college playoffs because he doesn't want to play us again," Ledbetter said. "He didn't want to play us again because we would've beat the shit out of them."

Instead it was Clemson that did so in the national championship. Georgia's season would not end in glory either. The Bulldogs lost convincingly to Texas in the Sugar Bowl. The 28–21 final score was not indicative. There was too much of a letdown factor for the Bulldogs, who also played without Baker, who sat out to preserve his first-round draft stock. Several injured starters sat out as well. "Honestly, we weren't up for that game," Ledbetter acknowledged. "We wanted the whole thing. It's bad to say we weren't in it, but our hearts weren't in the Sugar Bowl. Nothing to take away from Texas, they've got a great football team. They obviously proved that, but we honestly just didn't care. We knew where we should have been. We knew what should've happened. You can't really say that Alabama thing wasn't on our hearts still because it was. It's just not how we wanted to write our story."

Such as it was, that performance knocked Georgia's final ranking down to No. 7 in the final AP poll. Though it wasn't what anybody envisioned going into the SEC Championship Game, it was the second best final ranking for the program since 2012. A few months later, Jackson Harris, the senior tight end on that 2018 team, summed up how he saw that season.

"Just coming off that big loss [in the national championship], it's tough to end the season the way we did in 2017 and turn around and get it going good again," Harris said. "It's motivation. But it's also you get that close, and you see all the work you did, you tasted it, then you lost it. How we responded to that—obviously there are ups and downs throughout the season. But for the most part, we responded well."

Davis, the four-year starter, watched the 2018 team from afar. He also saw that season as a positive step even if it wasn't the championship that everyone craved. "It was a process that happened over the years, and we finally were able to get it right in 2017," Davis said. "And they showed that they were able to keep it right in 2018."

19

The 2019 Season

E VERYONE WAS IN A GREAT MOOD. IT WAS A FESTIVE day in the early hours of the second day of 2020, a year which had begun right for this Georgia football team. Players, staffers, and coaches were hugging on the field at the Superdome in New Orleans. They had corrected a wrong from last year and turned a loss on that field into a win this time. They had finished the season with a win, something that had not happened the previous two years. It was not exactly the game anyone had hoped to finish the season by winning, but it was a win—26–14 against Baylor in the Sugar Bowl—and everyone was relieved.

Kirby Smart was among the ecstatic. He let his guard down enough to even joke with the media, which had hoarded at the entrance to the locker room ready to invade and talk to everyone inside. On his way to the main press conference with two of his players, Smart turned to Jake Fromm and George Pickens, pointed at the reporters, and joked: "They don't wanna talk to us! We're not important!"

Smart was still in a great mood a few minutes later when he returned to the locker room.

"Who you hunting?" Smart asked me. He could tell I couldn't find the guy I was looking for. I told him, and Smart pointed me in the right direction.

It was a cheerful ending to the season. But even amidst all this, everyone, especially Smart, knew change would still be coming. For all his upbeat talk, Smart knew that changes needed to be made and he was about to make them.

* * *

The noon games are always the worst. When anyone looked back on Kirby Smart's first season at Georgia and those rough games that did not scream progress, they had a commonality: noon kickoffs. Vanderbilt. Georgia Tech. Nicholls State. Ole Miss. The first three were all at home. And so was this game three years later against South Carolina.

The Bulldogs had trudged from their hotel rooms to the team bus that took them to Sanford Stadium, then trudged into the locker room, and then trudged through warm-ups. Something was amiss. Smart could sense it. As he does before every game, Chuck Dowdle pulled up to Smart for the customary pregame coach's interview. This was normally a perfunctory session with two short questions and answers. But this time Smart—unlike his team—was amped up. "We gotta get our ass ready to play," Smart said. "Our team's not ready to play right now. We gotta get our team ready to play."

Dowdle later said he could never recall a coach saying that to him that close to the start of the game. And unfortunately for himself and his program, Smart would prove to have a perfect handle on the pulse of his team. This day also proved to be an important day for the program in an important year, though it wasn't as important as each of the first two years of the Smart era. Year One had been the installation of the culture change. Year Two had been the manifestation of it. But Year Three had been…what exactly? It was hard to say for sure. They had not quite built on things by winning it all. They had not even won the conference or gone back to the playoff. But they had not slipped enough—even after the embarrassing Sugar Bowl loss—for anyone to say the previous season was a fluke. The program still had too much going for it. But in the grand design of a program, you usually need two things to happen: the ultimate success or the necessary humbling to prevent complacency. Georgia did not really get either in Year Three. It did get that humbling in Year Four.

In fact, it got it twice. You could argue it got it off the field, too, in the form of the quarterback who critics carped (inaccurately) Georgia had let get away. That would be Justin Fields, who had given up on becoming Georgia's starting quarterback—at least given up on it happening soon enough for his tastes—and transferred to Ohio State, where he attained immediate eligibility through the smart efforts of Tom Mars, a lawyer experienced in pushing transfer cases in front of the NCAA. A Georgia baseball player yelled a racial epithet at a football game in reference to Fields, which was assumed to be the basis of the transfer, though Mars disputed that characterization. Either way, Fields got the request. And as anyone could have predicted when Fields, the former five-star prospect, joined an Ohio State offense perfectly tailored to his abilities, he had a great season. He put up big numbers, and the Buckeyes won the Big Ten and made the playoff.

Jake Fromm and Georgia, meanwhile, did not. And they did not because of their offense. The how and why for that could be debated for years. Was it the fault of new offensive coordinator James Coley, who was promoted into the play-calling role after Jim Chaney left for Tennessee? Was it the fault of Fromm, whose play seemed to regress, especially in that fateful October game against South Carolina? Was it the lack of experienced receivers after the unexpected summer dismissal of Jeremiah Holloman? Was it the vaunted offensive line and running game not being as good as expected? Or was it just a perfect storm of factors? In the end the drop was precipitous, and Georgia essentially wasted an unexpectedly great year from a young, star-laden defense. And it led to some humility.

First came South Carolina, which was an underdog by more than three touchdowns. Everything would have to go wrong for Georgia to lose. Everything did, seemingly. Fromm threw four interceptions, including a pick-six. The offense couldn't move the ball. Already down to its backup quarterback entering the game, South Carolina had to go to its No. 3 quarterback, a more mobile quarterback, which threw Georgia's defense for enough of a loop to get the game to overtime. And then in overtime, Rodrigo Blankenship missed a short field goal, sealing the loss. It was a stunning day. But it was not the final humiliation.

That came via LSU in the SEC Championship Game, when perhaps the more important lesson was rammed home: defense no longer wins championships. Everyone agreed that Georgia had the better defense. But LSU had a historically great offense and ran all over the Bulldogs, who for the first time in these four trips to Mercedes-Benz Stadium were not even competitive and lost 37–10.

For the first time in his tenure, Smart faced real questions and real criticism from his fanbase. It revolved around his management of the offense. His team had predictable play-calling (too many runs up the middle) and an old-school offense, while LSU and Alabama were slinging the ball around. The approach was given a derisive name —man ball—by popular blogger Michael Brochstein, who ran the blog, Get The Picture. The phrase began to catch on, and before long Smart himself was referring to it during the aftermath of the SEC Championship Game. "People can say, 'well, Coach Smart wants to play man ball,'" Smart said. "Coach Smart wants to win."

This would serve as an example of the two sides of Smart when under criticism. Publicly, he was defiant and defended and shielded his assistants and players. Privately, he was planning changes.

Some of it was foisted on Smart. Soon after the SEC Championship Game, offensive tackles Andrew Thomas and Isaiah Wilson turned pro. After the Sugar Bowl, two more linemen followed him out the door. Solomon Kindley also declared for the draft, and in an unexpected bombshell, Cade Mays transferred to Tennessee the same day a bizarre twist emerged. His father sued the school because he severed a pinky on a chair during a recruiting visit. (These stories tend to only happen in the SEC.)

Smart also finally lost Sam Pittman, who got the head coaching job at Arkansas. Pittman had been one of Smart's first and most important hires and he gave the program four great years. But as with any good assistant, it's inevitable they will leave for better jobs, and the trick is to replace them well. Smart ended up getting lucky this time. Matt Luke, recently fired as Ole Miss head coach, was available, and Smart quickly swooped in to make him Pittman's replacement. That was as close to an even swap as one could get.

D'Andre Swift also turned pro after the Sugar Bowl. That was expected. But a couple of other departures in the early days of 2020 changed the course of the program and showed how willing Smart was to deviate from his public persona. Fromm had retreated to the woods after the Sugar Bowl to mull his future. And when he emerged, he was a former Georgia quarterback. After three years the Bulldogs definitely needed a new starter. Smart and Coley had long known this was a possibility and had privately prepared a list of potential replacements. A few days before the Sugar Bowl and even before Fromm made his decision, the name of Wake Forest starter Jamie Newman appeared in the transfer portal. A dual-threat quarterback, Newman was a grad transfer, making him immediately eligible. Smart and Coley got in touch with Newman as soon as they could and stayed in touch. Oregon was one of the schools hot on Newman's trail, but the North Carolina native waited to see what Fromm would do.

Fromm announced his departure on a Wednesday. By Friday Newman was enrolled at Georgia. When he announced his decision, he referred to playing for Smart and Coley. And yet even after adding Newman there was another one: JT Daniels, a former five-star quarterback in the 2018 class, opted to transfer from USC to Georgia. It was another sign of Smart's determination to load up, especially at the game's most important position. Daniels' addition proved fortuitous. Newman shocked the program in early September by opting out just weeks before the start of the season.

But by this time, another situation was brewing. Scott Fountain, the special teams coordinator, had left to join Pittman's staff at Arkansas. That provided Smart an opportunity. Back in early 2005 before he began his one-year stint on Mark Richt's staff at Georgia, Smart had been a holdover at LSU, working there for a few weeks during the transition from Nick Saban to Les Miles. The new LSU staff included a young receivers coach named Todd Monken.

Monken had gone on to the NFL, then back to college, and then back to the NFL. He was now available after a year as the offensive coordinator for the dysfunctional Cleveland Browns. Monken's reputation was that of a sharp offensive mind, one who could open things up with the passing game while not sacrificing the running game. His hiring would be a coup for Georgia. The only problem was there was no opening for an offensive coordinator at Georgia, and Smart and Coley were close.

But business is business. Smart made the move, trying to soften the blow for Coley by saying he would remain as assistant head coach. But Coley, understandably, decided to move on, hooking back up with former boss Jimbo Fisher at Texas A&M.

Smart still wasn't done because Coley's departure had meant another opportunity. And this time Smart was going to throw a real curveball. Four years before, Scott Cochran had been on the verge of leaving Alabama for Georgia to become the strength and conditioning coordinator for his close friend. But Cochran had been talked out of it by Nick Saban. He spent the next four years in Tuscaloosa, burnishing his reputation as perhaps the best at his job in college football, even doing commercials with Saban. But Cochran was getting antsy; he was 40 years old and not satisfied with being a legendary strength coach the rest of his professional life. He wanted to get an assistant coaching job, and his old friend in Athens had an opening.

Smart moved stealthily, so stealthily that even some of his other assistants had no idea this was brewing. Even some close to the program, who usually are privy to information, were caught off guard. It was a bold risk for Georgia but a shot across the bow at Alabama. The two SEC programs had finished No. 1 and No. 2 in the recruiting rankings for the 2020 class.

Smart had overhauled his offense—partly in reaction to events and partly on his own initiative. He had stolen away one of Alabama's top assets. He did it without a grand speech or a huge press conference. It did not guarantee that everything was fixed. But it did reinforce what should have already been apparent about Georgia football under Smart: he would never sit on his hands.

* * *

Loran Smith's office is tucked in a corner at the Butts-Mehre building. The door is usually open. There is memorabilia everywhere, including books, programs, and pictures. But above all there is Smith's institutional memory. One day, well into Smart's tenure, we sat talking about how eerily similar Kirby Smart and Mark Richt's first few years had gone.

They both won eight games in Year One. They both won 13 games and an SEC championship in Year Two. They both won 11 games in Year Three. They had similar records (12–2 for Smart and 10–2 for Richt) in Year Four. The feeling around both was also the same. Expectations rose in the fanbase, assuming that a powerhouse would be built and the young head coach would be around for a long time.

Of course, Richt stayed around 11 more years but never delivered that national championship. It turns out he had already produced his best season in terms of number of wins. (He'd win one more SEC championship, a dozen games one more time, and double-digit wins six more times.)

So I asked Smith what made Smart different this time. This was no rabid Richt critic. Smith had just visited Richt in Miami a month before and liked and admired him. But like many writers, Smith had ended up believing that Richt just wasn't enough of a "hard ass" to win it all, especially in the day and age dominated by Nick Saban. Being a hard ass, though, wasn't just what allowed to Saban build a dynasty at Alabama. It was the organization, the culture he had instilled. Not all of Saban's assistants had been able to replicate that when they became head coaches. Smart had done that in those first three years at Georgia, at least from an organizational and cultural standpoint. Smith, who had known and observed so many others, marveled at Smart as the complete package. "He's just got a grasp of everything," Smith said. "But having said that, it doesn't mean it's going to guarantee you a championship. But I've always felt that to win a championship, Kirby is doing the things you've gotta do. He's the best I've ever seen."

Smith spoke in the late afternoon a couple weeks after 2019's spring practice had ended.

"But I say that with a little disclaimer: Vince [Dooley]'s record was pretty good," Smith said. "But I don't think Vince was as comfortable with people as Kirby...[Dooley] was 31 years old when he got the job at Georgia. He just wasn't as relaxed and comfortable. He acquired that trait later on. But Kirby's just got marvelous instincts."

Ray Goff, the old Georgia coach who still lived in Athens, could only look at all that had happened and how the program had been elevated under the kid he had recruited. He marveled at it. "When he came in, he took over for Coach Richt. And Mark, I loved Mark Richt, I think he's a great guy, but Kirby he came in and he changed things around a little bit," Goff said. "I have a tremendous amount of respect for Mark. Sometimes when you have a change in leadership or a boss or different things, sometimes it just works. And I know people say, 'Well, that's stupid.' It probably is. But there's just different times, and things just click. And I think Kirby, he clicked in a big way at Georgia."

Jonathan Ledbetter brought up the culture that had been built at Georgia. "They're going to be year in and year out successful," Ledbetter told me, "because it's not just who they're recruiting. That has something to do with it, but the people that are recruiting know what kind of culture they're getting into, and they know what's expected of them and they know what the standard is. And the standard is to win football games and to be a beast, on the field, off the field, everywhere. Be a beast. Be a shark. Wake up eating. Eat everything. Eat the books. Eat the nutrition. Eat the field. Eat the studying. Eat it all. And that's how he breeds everything, breeds everyone. And that's never going to change.

"As long as he's there, that's never changing."

Acknowledgments

Davin Bellamy met me for lunch on a cold, rainy day and he was battling a cold. But he still sat in a booth at a sports bar with me for two hours and remembered his Georgia career, sharing stories. The best memories. The bad ones.

Jeb Blazevich did the same with me one afternoon in downtown Atlanta. He was there for the bachelor party of another former Georgia tight end, Jackson Harris, who stopped by near the end of our talk and shared his own memories.

Shane Beamer called me during an eight-hour drive with his family, recounting his own two years on Kirby Smart's staff. When I asked if his family would be annoyed listening to his end of the conversation, he laughed. "Nah, the kids have their iPads and earphones on. We're good." We spoke for two hours.

I couldn't have done this book without the help of the above people or the others who were so generous with their time: Jonathan Ledbetter, Kevin Butler, Aaron Davis, Chuck Dowdle, Loran Smith, as well as a couple sources who shall go nameless for various reasons. I also need to thank Claude Felton, the inimitable Georgia communications director, who was among the first people I told about this book project and who was helpful to me at several turns. The majority of the reporting of this book came from direct interviews I did, but articles by Pete Thamel for Yahoo.com, Wilson Alexander for TheRed&Black.com, Will Leitch for SportsonEarth.com, and Vince Dooley's book, *Dooley: My 40 Years at Georgia*, were immensely helpful.

But the biggest thanks are reserved for two groups of people:

1. My family, especially my wife, who gave me the time for this endeavor, including three days of my own holed up in a hotel near the Atlanta airport with nothing but the charge to: "Finish this damn book."

2. Georgia fans.

Credit also to my mother-in-law, Doris Gerst, who not only told me I should write the book, but also ordered her daughter to let me write it. And credit to my parents, who although not major sports fans still indulged and encouraged my love for sports as a kid. (Obviously I never outgrew it. Who does?)

The team at Triumph Books has also been a joy to deal with, especially my editor Jeff Fedotin. They made my first publishing experience as easy as possible.

When Triumph Books asked me to write the book, it was because they thought there would be a market for this story, and my response to that was: "You have no idea."

I'm not a Georgia native, having come to the state at the tender age of 26, but I've been around long enough to see what a unique and passionate group this is. The rest of the country found that out over the years covered in this book—whether it was the takeover of Notre Dame Stadium, the trip to the Rose Bowl, or other en masse trips to bewildered road cities.

Georgia fans are like Boston Red Sox fans pre-2004 or Chicago Cubs fans pre-2016, and I mean that in the best of ways. The reason the nation latched on to the plight of those fanbases is because there were so many of them, and Georgia has that, too, albeit without quite the length of misery. In fact, there has been quite a lot of winning since 1980. Just not enough.

Smart has brought Georgia pretty close, however. And his connection to this story makes it a bit personal for me, too, in a roundabout way. His first full-time college job was in south Georgia at Valdosta State. My first job in this state was also in south Georgia at *The Albany Herald*, where I covered Valdosta State. I missed Smart by a season, but three years later when he returned to be on Mark Richt's staff, he called me—Claude Felton told him to—and we briefly shared some Valdosta memories before moving on to talk about Smart's new gig.

Fourteen years later Felton again put Smart and I together to talk about Valdosta for a story I was writing for The Athletic. By this time in his career, Smart was the hard-charging, jaded, guarded, multi-millionaire head coach. But in that talk he turned back into the young kid getting his start at Valdosta, the kid humbled by the job, the kid who didn't forget where he came from.

Much of this book is based on my own experience and perspective, my job giving me a front-row seat to the Smart era at Georgia. I don't know how the story will end. I don't know how long the story will last. I hope I did a decent enough job presenting this part of the story. And I'm eager to see where it goes from here.